Robinson Jeffers Family Travel Diaries

Volume One

British Isles, 1929

Family Passport Photograph, 1929. Clockwise from top left, Garth, Donnan, Una, and Robinson. Photograph by Lewis Josselyn.

Robinson Jeffers Family Travel Diaries

Volume One

British Isles, 1929

Edited by Deborah Whittlesey Sharp

With Contributions by Donnan Jeffers
and Robert Kafka

Tor House Press
Carmel, California

Tor House Press
Carmel, California

ISBN hardcover: 978-0-9622774-4-3
ISBN paperback: 978-0-9622774-3-6

Library of Congress Cataloguing-in-Publication Data available on
request.

Contents

Page 24 of the original 1929 Jeffers Family Travel Diary.

Introduction
Deborah Whittlesey Sharp

In the late summer or early fall of 1927 Robinson Jeffers began
mentioning "vague" plans afoot for a family trip to Ireland,
Scotland, and perhaps Italy. The timing of those plans made
sense. It was three years since Jeffers' self-publication of *Tamar
and Other Poems* had introduced him to the literary world and
two years since he received national acclaim with the Boni &
Liveright publication of *Roan Stallion, Tamar and Other Poems*. It
was also two years after he finished building Hawk Tower for
his wife Una, inspired by her love of the medieval Irish round
towers.

But Robinson showed little enthusiasm for travel or
Ireland. He made it clear that he was absolutely content with
life at Tor House with Una and their twin sons, Donnan and
Garth. He wrote to John Varney in 1927, "It is time no doubt
to see the world a little, but here are the ocean and the rock
and my trees growing up . . . it is hard to make the decision."
And in his September 13, 1928, letter to Mark Van Doren,
presumably in answer to a question from him, Robinson wrote
"—Why Ireland? I hardly know: it rains in summer as well as
winter, & there are gray stones in the fields." But he knew of
Una's love for her ancestral home, her prodigious
organizational skills, and her will. He probably already sensed
the trip was inevitable.

Indeed, as Robinson had already reported to Van Doren in May of 1928, Una had been leasing houses in Ireland and Scotland by letter, and she had established a fund earmarked for Ireland. Into that fund went a check from friend and patron Albert Bender, born in Dublin of German parents and raised there until he was fifteen. He was a founder of the San Francisco-based Book Club of California, which published 310 copies of a special signed edition of *Poems* by Robinson Jeffers. In his October 8, 1928, letter to Robinson, Bender wrote, "I . . . enclose check for $150 as compensation for the bothersome task of signing the edition." Una responded immediately, "As to the check that is just a gift from the gods— . . . I have put [it] into our *Ireland fund.* —you see it will have a proper use eventually."

Bender took notice. In Christmas greetings to the Jefferses that year, Bender included a check for a significant sum of money for the trip, so significant, in fact, that both Una and Robinson at first felt it wrong to accept the gift. In his letter of thanks to Bender, however, Robinson wrote, "Over night we have both thought gratefully that you really wanted us to have it; and it will be used for no other purpose than the Irish journey."

And so the trip was finally launched, Una fully aware of the effort involved. In January of 1929 she wrote to Barnet B. Ruder, "—It is rather a business taking R. J. a-travelling. I think in his heart he feels he has done enough of it, — but once we get there all will be well . . . ." And it was. The diary the family kept attests to the journey's success.

*   *   *   *

This publication of the Jefferses' 1929 travel diary is not the first transcription of the material. The first transcribers were the family themselves, and they began the task while they were still traveling. The transcription was written in the same kind of school exercise books as the original diary. On the inside cover of the first volume, Una wrote: "Fair & true copy in ink of original Diary. Copy was begun at 'Kerry Vor,' Britwell Salome near Watlington Oxfordshire, England. Pages 36–80 copied on board Canadian Pacific 'Duchess of Bedford' sailed from Belfast Dec. 10, 1929 for New York."

The transcription, however, was not entirely "true." In the entries Una copied she occasionally made slight revisions: sometimes small omissions of words or phrases and sometimes additions that must have come to mind as she recopied the diary. She also looked over the work of the other members of the family and made occasional slight revisions in pencil. Over the years, Una also transcribed the diaries she and the family kept of their two additional journeys to Ireland, in 1937 and 1948.

In 1954, four years after Una's death, the Ward Ritchie Press in Los Angeles published *Visits to Ireland: Travel-Diaries of Una Jeffers*, a beautifully produced, limited edition, small volume of excerpts from the 1929 diary, chosen by Robinson from the "fair & true" copy. The poet also wrote a foreword for the edition, which appears in this volume.

Donnan was inspired by the reception of *Visits to Ireland* to prepare a transcription of the complete Irish portions of all the diaries the family kept, including the diary he kept during the trip in 1956 that he made with his wife Lee, their two young children, Lindsay and Una, and Robinson. His goal was to give the diaries a much wider audience, and by 1971 he had completed a typescript of the Irish portions of all four trips. The original diaries are sometimes difficult to decipher, particularly the 1929 diary, written as it was by four people, two of them only twelve years old, often in pencil, in ruled copy books. Sometimes the writing is nearly illegible; sometimes a writer goes back to an earlier entry and adds to it, writing in the margins; sometimes entries are interrupted by notes written earlier on pages that were still blank. It's not surprising, then, that Donnan appears to have used the fair copies as the basis for his transcriptions, but he continued to modify them, correcting punctuation and often adding or subtracting from the fair copy texts, giving them a more polished, refined voice.

Donnan died before he was able to publish the diaries, so when it was decided to pursue that goal, Robert Kafka, past secretary-treasurer of the Robinson Jeffers Association, and his wife Kyuja took on the job of preparing Donnan's transcriptions for publication. Rob retained Donnan's edits, corrections, and explanatory notes and added notes of his own. He also procured a scan of the original diaries held by the Harry Ransom Center at the University of Texas at Austin, and from them transcribed the Scottish and English portions of the 1929 journey, retaining Donnan's preference for a polished style.

I joined the project when it was decided to hew more closely to the original diaries. Having Rob's manuscript of Donnan's transcription of the Irish portion of the 1929 journey and his own transcription of the Scottish and English portions gave me a running start on producing a new, exact transcript of the original 1929 diary, putting back the elements Donnan had smoothed away, including his own twelve-year-old phonetic spellings and Una's slap-dash punctuation and sometimes fragmented sentences. The result of that effort is this publication. The diaries of the 1937, 1948, and 1956 journeys will follow later, each a transcription faithful to the original diaries. By remaining faithful to the originals, the vitality of the diaries is preserved. Their value lies in the distinctive characteristics of each writer and the personalities those characteristics reveal.

Una was the primary contributor to the diaries. Her energy and enthusiasm; her sure, bold hand and use of dashes; her infrequent use of conventional punctuation, especially apostrophes; her quick mind and extensive knowledge and love of things Irish fill the majority of the entries. Her likes and dislikes and her vivid emotions are very evident.

Robinson's personality and reactions are very apparent as well. His entries, in his crabbed hand, are more deliberate and carefully written. He observes landscapes and, of course, he observes stones—both natural and those worked by ancient peoples—with the eye of a stonemason. His observations of people sometimes include snippets of conversation written with attention to the speaker's accent and manner of speech, and his detailed, skilled drawings appear throughout the diary.

The twins make their own very distinctive contributions. Donnan's frequent entries in a not yet formed hand, characterized by his own unique spellings, reveal his interest in weaponry and war and an enthusiasm for recording details of the family's travels. Garth's entries, in his already well-formed, careful hand, reveal his love of and fascination with animals and birds.

I have attempted to retain all these qualities by keeping all the stylistic quirks of the writers, including slap-dash punctuation and creative spelling. My aim was to give readers as much as possible a reading experience similar to mine. As I read the original diaries, I quickly forgot their roughness and instead became caught up in the personalities of the writers; their discoveries of the Irish, Scottish, and English countrysides, towns, and cities they motored through; the things that interested each writer; and the distinctive descriptions of each. Una's entries are often quite lyrical; Robinson's, thoughtful and measured. In Donnan's and Garth's are hints of their developing personalities: Donnan as chatty and animated as his mother; Garth, more like his reserved father. And overarching all, there is the sense of a close-knit family discovering new places together in a memorable, marathon, seven-month journey.

*   *   *   *

First and foremost, I would like to thank Robinson Jeffers Tor House Foundation Trustees James Karman (Emeritus Professor, California State University, Chico) and Norris Pope (former Director, Stanford University Press) for their guidance and support. Norris designed the book, cover-to-cover, typeset its contents, including the detailed and unconventional diary text, with unerring expertise and care, and shepherded the manuscript through the printing process. James offered his extensive knowledge, experience, and wisdom throughout the entire process. Without Norris and James, this publication would never have come to be.

Tor House Foundation president Elliot Ruchowitz-Roberts is also responsible for this volume. His enthusiasm for the project, and his support of the Tor House Press in particular, helped to make this publication possible. All of us involved with the Foundation appreciate his efforts to creatively perpetuate the legacy of Robinson Jeffers.

Foundation Administrative Assistant Melinda Bowman Manlin was a faithful and meticulous proofreader of several drafts and the index. I appreciated tremendously her willingness to deal with the unusual manuscript and difficult-to-read original text of the diary.

Paula Karman's oversight of the index was indispensable; I could not have done without her editorial expertise, sharp eye, and patient guidance.

Alan Stacy, Foundation photo archivist and Trustee, worked magic enhancing Una's snapshots. They add significantly to this edition.

Joan Hendrickson, former Foundation photo archivist and cataloguer of the travel diary photos, offered valuable advice and ideas. Her continued interest in Tor House and her archival expertise are important to the Foundation and this project.

Finally, I would like to thank the Interpretation Team at Edinburgh Castle for sending me the exact wording of Mary, Queen of Scots' prayer which Una copied during the family's visit to the Castle.

Notes on the Transcription

Defining Approach

As mentioned earlier, every effort has been made to present the Jeffers family's 1929 travel diary as it was originally written, including errors in spelling and punctuation. Retaining those errors adds to the authenticity of the text and to the accurate representation of the four contributors to the diary.

Editorial Devices

abc	italic	*single underline*
abc	bold italic	***more than one underline***
~~abc~~	strikethrough	~~words or letters crossed out~~
{abc}	curved brackets	{words written in margins}
[abc]	square brackets	[material provided by editor]
[ ]	empty square brackets	[illegible words]

Initials of family members are added in the left margin at the beginnings of dated entries to indicate the initiator of the entry.

If a new writer adds material within an entry begun by another writer, the initials of the new writer are added in square brackets immediately before his or her added material.

UJ   Una Jeffers

RJ   Robinson Jeffers

DJ   Donnan Jeffers

GJ   Garth Jeffers

Notations for Journeys by Car

For each of their journeys by car, the family kept a list of the cities, towns, and important villages that they passed through. The places where they spent the night are underlined; the places where they ate dinner are followed by a superscript x; and the places where they saw round towers are followed by a superscript o. (See Una's July 12th entry, p. 18. See also pp. 28-29, 40, 69–71, and 117–18.)

Identification of People

Whenever possible, brief identifications have been provided in footnotes for people referred to in the diary by their first or last names only. Identifications have not been provided for those whose whole names appear within the text. Readers wanting fuller identification of friends and relations of the Jefferses should consult the indexes of *The Collected Letters of Robinson Jeffers, with Selected Letters of Una Jeffers*, edited by James Karman.

Glossary

byre: a cowshed.

Cahir: an Irish name meaning "warrior."

cairn: a heap of stones set up as a monument, landmark, or tomb.

cairngorm: a piece of smoky quartz found especially in parts of Scotland.

coign: a projecting corner, a cornerstone, an angle.

cromlech: a megalithic chamber tomb; dolmen.

fosse: a moat or defensive ditch in a fortification, usually filled with water; any ditch, trench, or canal.

garth: an open courtyard enclosed by a cloister; a yard or garden.

hooker: any fishing vessel working with hooks and lines rather than nets.

leads: a roof, especially one that is shallow or flat, covered with lead.

xvi   *Glossary*

loaning: an uncultivated plot of farmland, usually used for milking cows.

lough: a lake; loch.

Orpington: one of a breed of large, white-skinned chickens.

rath: a strong, usually circular earthen wall forming an enclosure and serving as a fort and residence for a tribal chief.

Sambur: a deer, of India, southeastern Asia, the East Indies, and the Philippines, having three-pointed antlers.

skene dhu: a small knife tucked into the top of a stocking in the full dress of a Scottish Highlander.

sporran: in Scottish Highlander dress, a large pouch, commonly of fur, worn suspended from a belt in front of the kilt.

torque: a collar, necklace, or similar ornament consisting of a twisted narrow band, usually of precious metal, worn especially by the ancient Gauls and Britons.

tumulus: an artificial mound, especially over a grave; barrow.

List of Photographs

Frontispiece. Family Passport Photograph, 1929. Clockwise from top left, Garth, Donnan, Una, and Robinson. Photograph by Lewis Josselyn; Tor House Foundation Archive.

Page vi. Page 24 of the original 1929 Jeffers Family Travel Diary. Harry Ransom Center, University of Texas at Austin.

Page xx. Page 1 of the original 1929 Jeffers Family Travel Diary. Harry Ransom Center, University of Texas at Austin.

A photo section follows p. 166. Captions for the photographs are based on the notes written by Una Jeffers on the backs of the prints.

1. Donnan, Robinson, and Garth on board ship near Greenock, Scotland. Gift of Brenda Jeffers, Tor House Foundation Archive; © Robinson Jeffers Tor House Foundation.

2. Donnan and Garth in Gort, Ireland, August. Gift of Brenda Jeffers, Tor House Foundation Archive; © Robinson Jeffers Tor House Foundation.

3. Moore Hall, near Castlebar, Co. Mayo, Ireland. Gift of Brenda Jeffers, Tor House Foundation Archive; © Robinson Jeffers Tor House Foundation.

4. Robinson, Donnan, and Garth at the Giant's Causeway, Northern Ireland. Gift of Brenda Jeffers, Tor House Foundation Archive; © Robinson Jeffers Tor House Foundation.

5. Edward Martyn's Tillyra Castle, near Kiltartan, Co. Galway, Ireland. Gift of Brenda Jeffers, Tor House Foundation Archive; © Robinson Jeffers Tor House Foundation.

6. Donnan, Garth, and Una, Cushendun, Glens of Antrim, Ireland. Gift of Brenda Jeffers, Tor House Foundation Archive; © Robinson Jeffers Tor House Foundation.

7. Yeats' Tower at Ballylee Castle, Ireland, July. Gift of Brenda Jeffers, Tor House Foundation Archive; © Robinson Jeffers Tor House Foundation.

8. Garth and Donnan in churchyard, Clonmacnoise, Ireland. Gift of Brenda Jeffers, Tor House Foundation Archive; © Robinson Jeffers Tor House Foundation.

Robinson Jeffers Family Travel Diaries

Volume One

British Isles, 1929

Page 1 of the original 1929 Jeffers Family Travel Diary.

Vol I.   fair and Calm evening.
Thursday June 6.   I should say cloudy, for we when about sun a red ba...

Left our darling Tor House today and started on
our long journey to the British Isles — and back!
Left after a day of strenuous labors getting things
in order to leave for a year — getting ourselves
packed — all kinds of clothes for four people
for town & country — Cold wet and hot —
Our chickens were sent down to Edith at Fn
Tana to board — Pigeons given to Yasitaka Myunto
in the ranch by the mission orchard. Mrs Skene
& Mrs Odell came to say goodbye & Weather and
Prayer, Jimmie Hopper Kindly took us to the
station at Monterey, left at 6:42 PM. Passed
gorgeous colored acres of sweet peas and na-
sturtiums — these we saw being threshed last
year — strange & old worldly, horses tramp-
ling the seed pods on great outspread
tarpaulins.   We look like nice
travellers!

1929

UJ Thursday June 6. *Fair* and calm evening.

[**RJ**] I should say cloudy, fair and calm. Late sun a red ball.

[**UJ**] Left our darling Tor House today, and started on our long journey to the British Isles—and back! Left after a day of strenuous labors getting things in order to leave for a year—getting ourselves packed—all kinds of clothes for four people for town & country—cold wet and hot— Our chickens were sent down to Edith at Fontana to board. Pigeons given to Yasitaka Miyamoto[1] in the ranch by the mission orchard. Mrs Skene and Mrs Odell came to say goodbye & Mattie and Praeger.[2] Jimmie Hopper kindly took us to the station at Monterey, left at 6:42 PM. Passed gorgeous colored acres of sweet peas and nasturtiums—these we saw being threshed last year—strange & old worldly, horses trampling the seed pods on great outspread tarpaulins. We look like nice travellers!

[**RJ**] San Francisco, on the station platform came a woman to Garth and Donnan. "Are you twins? I was looking for you." Una asked her to explain, she said she was a Travelers' Aid officer, and had received a wire, unsigned, telling her to meet twins, twelve years old. Una said she couldn't spare the boys,

---

[1] The Tor House chickens and pigeons were left in the care of Edith Allan, Una's older half-sister, and Yositaka Miyamoto, a 15-year-old friend of Garth and Donnan who lived nearby.

[2] The farewell party included friends and neighbors Charlotte Skene, Ruth Odell, Mattie Hopper, and Bessie or Harry Praeger. Robinson's younger brother Hamilton and friend Albert Bender said good-bye in San Francisco.

and the woman left, with reluctance and suspicion. Can any one of our friends have attempted a ~~practical~~-joke? Street-car to Sutter Hotel.

DJ Friday, June 7   Cloudy—fair—rain—cold from snow on mountain.
Uncle Hamilton and Albert Bender came to the Sutter to see us off. In the ferry bulding there was a large reliefe map of California, it was very interesting. We went across the bay on the Sacramento, at Suisun the train was devided into pieces and ferried across the bay to Benicia. Going through Sacramento we caught a short glimpse of the Capitol. There were alot of long snow slids and tunneles. Alot of snow in the mountains.
[**GJ**] In the same car with us are another pair of twins, girls, they too are going to Europe for the first time. We found lots of similarities in our lives. As we passed Donner Lake we contrasted in our minds the conditions of 80 years ago with those of the present day. When we passed Dutch Flats we saw some of the old wood and adobe houses the miners lived in.
[**UJ**] In drawing room next to ours Mrs George friend of Effie Fortune.[3]

GJ Saturday June 8th, Fair Temp. 80 (tiny crescent moon).
The country is very desolate along here as a whole, sagebrush and alkalid flats. We crossed the Great Salt Lake today at about eleven oclock. Mother wrote ten letters. At one station I got off to see a queer looking pigeon which could fly about as well as a chicken. Later on in the day while we were going through Wyoming we saw alot of very interesting rock formations. Nearly all the time we could see some snow-clad peaks in one direction or another. [**UJ**] We have been interested to see the air mail beacons on high mts & cliffs shooting their rays out over desolate regions.

---

[3] E. Charlotte "Effie" Fortune was an artist who lived in Monterey.

DJ Sunday, June 9th Hot Temp.—88–90.
Kept the fan going all day. Country practicly the same all day, rolling plains mostly planted with grain with here and there little red farm houses and barns, [**RJ**] some of cut stone. Missouri River. Temp. 84 at midnight.

UJ Monday June 10 Hot arrived Chicago 9:00 cooler. Breakfast at Mich. Cent. Depot after a ride in Parmalee bus across city. Train at 10:30, Jackson 3:30 met by Daisy Jerry Mamma in 2 cars.[4] Lovely ride home & fine supper at the Arbor. Lots of talk. Daisy's house very comfortable & pretty. Mammas place too lots of improvements & all spick & span. Country beautiful. Cool & pleasant.

UJ Tues June 11 Zelle came. Long talk about our lives and her little boy who died. Went to Maxie's after lunch & stayed for supper. Max looks very ill, Gawn old too and a bit queer. Max had a lovely supper & everything nice. Took boys around place & in the barn. Contrary to the general idea—things look bigger to me than as a child—lane wider etc. —
[**DJ**] Today Uncle Jerry took us up to the top of the capitol at Lansing. We went up by elevator, all kinds of stairs and ladders until we reached the very top there we wrote our names. We had a wourndaful view all around the city. [**GJ**] In Lansing Uncle Jerry took us to Potters Park where there is a zoo. In it we saw a lot of animals—Lions, Leopards, coyotes, bears, bison etc.

---

[4] While in Mason, the Jefferses spent time with Una's relatives and friends: her mother Isabelle; twin sisters Daisy (wife of Jerry Bartley) and Violet (fiancée of Neil Hinkley); childhood companion Zelle (Moody) Bishop; Aunt Margaret "Max" Lindsay and Uncle Gawn Lindsay; Jason and Jessie Cross, with their daughter Estelle (Cross) Gildart and their son Paul; Zelle's parents George and Jennie Moody; and Julia (Minar) Freshour and her daughters Martha and Lana.

UJ Wed June 12, Rested in morning. Breakfast in bed. In P.M. Max came—then went to see Mr & Mrs Cross & Stella & Paul came then to Arbor for dinner & to Moody's. Evening Violets Neal came. Boys all practiced shooting at target & Daisy too. ~~Wood~~ mourning doves & bob whites called constantly at grandmothers. {Visited Papa's grave. We saw some fine old carved tombstones carved by some person apparently dated 1870–1880. Covered with lichen.}

UJ Thurs. June 13. Rain. Breakfast at Daisy's. Julia Minar & her 2 daughters came. Jerry took boys to manual training & they worked at arrows. Lunch at Mammas. Rain. Jerry took us to Jackson to train at 1:43. Mamma went too. D & G going to Cadillac tonight to get Violet. Got on to very crowded train. Very uncomfortable until we got compartment at Windsor. Went under the Detroit river to Canadian side in a tunnel.

DJ Friday. June 14 dim sunshine
Got to Montreal at nine. Took taxi to pier. A tug pulled us out of the dock and we started down the river. [**UJ**] Our "Dominion Overseas Limited" Train was very late. Mad scramble at pier about luggage. [**DJ**] At about eight P.M. a tug came out from Quebec and took the mail off. We saw fort Quebec on the hights. dull grey. There were six cannon outlined against the sky. We saw a large and imposing looking bulding that looked like a medieeval castle. Mother thought it was the Chateau Frontenac.

DJ Saturday June 15. Cold and foggy— Temp 50° Cold and sunshiny.
Got up at seven and had a sault-water-bath. We are passing the cost of ~~Newfoundland~~ New Brunswick. Got our stemer chares today and stayed in them quite a lot. In the ~~after~~ forenoon we had some bouillon which warmed us up. [**UJ**] & tea in the afternoon. This ship is clean & fresh and the meals are excellent. [**DJ**] We had drill to put on our cork jackets. We all

hastened to muster station "C." Here an officer was instructing the people "Five a-deep please—five a-deep."

GJ Sunday June 16 Cold with dense fog. Temp 48

Got up at seven and had another salt water bath. It was so cold that some sailors put up a tarpaulin along the side of the promenade. The whistle was kept blowing constantly because of the fog. About five oclock mother noticed that the propeller had stopped and called our attention to it pretty soon almost everybody started gathering on deck and looking over the rail. Knowing that we had had to go 140 miles out of our course on account of icebergs we thought it might be one that was causing us to stop. In a few minutes we felt a hard trembling under our feet and realized the ship was reversing its propeller. Pretty soon our ship began tooting its fog horn and was answered by four or five small horns in several directions. After about five minutes they all grew fainter and our ship started on its course again it turned out we had run into the middle of a fleet of fishing vessels. While the propeller was reversing a sailor pulled in the log line to prevent the current from sucking it into the propeller. The thing on the end was about a foot long and looked like a miniature torpedoe with slanting fins.

DJ Monday, June 17 Cold and foggy Temp. 40° while passing iceberg off Cape Race

The fog was so thick last night that the ship hove to from midnight to seven oclock this morning. About noon the fog cleared up. At three we sighted an iceberg, a little white spek on the horizon. At four we passed another iceberg about a mile away, we could see it very plainly. We had a lot of fun playing shuffleboard for the first time today. [UJ] The iceberg was dazzlingly white and beautiful in the oblique sunlight of late afternoon but O how terrifying so cold & dead and alone and unassailable and menacing—

Two nice Scotch elderly spinsters are opposite us at table B &

V Angus of Aberdeen. We are lucky to have them. Served us today with their own tea in their own chunky little travelled tea pot. They are pure type of upright Scotch. Very self respecting and honest and *convinced*.

DJ Tuesday, June 18 cold and grey with some rain.
The ship lay to again from 10 P.M. to 10 A.M. Today was the first time the ship rolled very much. We went to a horse race today. They were little wooden horses that people moved. They determined how far to move them by dice.

DJ Wednesday, June 19 foggy but not as cold
We went to the horse racing again today. We don't bet but we found that if we had we would have won almost every time.
[**UJ**] Distance each day so far. miles 376½, 373, 246, 221, 363, 375.
Mother has been reading "The Sundering Flood" by Wm Morris. —Garth & Donnan "Grapes of Wrath"[5] "From the Earth to the Moon" by Jules Verne. Father "Ireland" by Stephen Gwynn & "Ulster" by St. John Irvine.

UJ Thursday [June 20] foggy. Lay in berths part of day. Father reading aloud "Redcliffe," a Devon story by Eden Phillpotts.

UJ Friday June 21 foggy, part of day sunshine
Very fine *au revoir* dinner tonight. Boys went on tour of upper decks with party. Watched our Captain pace his deck. Firm & grim & commanding. Watched *following* waves—high and fast. Heard there was one stowaway found and put to work. Heard story of that old tragic wife & heavy stupid husband whom we called French Canadians. They have lived on far away ranch in Saskatchewan. Fearful years there—a life time her three children died improper treatment etc—husband brutal &

---

[5]A novel about World War I written by Boyd Cable (Ernest Andrew Ewart), published 1917.

bestial— now *she* has been left a fortune in Scotland and are on their way to claim it, he is now very attentive to her but she evidently hates him, says she hopes he will go back to Canada but she never will. Palmistry yesterday by Miss Angus. Few nice hours on deck.

UJ Sat, June 22 Yesterday was the summer solstice but we were the men in the street! 357 miles today, Irish coast in sight then the Scottish coast rough rugged many towers & lighthouses & at least one castle. Sunshine part of the day. Just learned that we were almost into an iceberg one night as we lay-to in the thick fog. The engines had to reverse very quickly to avoid it as it floated by. —Greenock tonight—many lights. The daylight lasted until ten at night. A beautiful beautiful sight were the sea gulls following the ship and flying about around the bow and the stern.

RJ Sunday, June 23. Horrible noises of luggage and conversation all night, the people excited to be in harbor, but I managed to open the port-hole, then we could close the cabin-door. No bath, the Clyde-water's too dirty. Scotch as a picture, the sharp gable-chimneyed houses of Greenock. Ben Lomond and Loch Fyne, but more excitement among the deck-standers for Harry Lauder's house. Now we are sliding across to Ireland; the ship has an extraordinary list to port. [**GJ**] The afternoon passed very slowly until Father began to read then it seemed scarcely any time before the tender came alongside. We had high tea while the trunks were being put aboard. After high tea we got on board the tender and sat on a bench near the bow, but the wind was so cold during the hour of waiting before the tender started that we went into the cabin just a few minutes after it left the Melita. About 30 minutes later we started going by the shipbuilding yards for which Belfast is famous. We got off the tender, and after the customs officer had looked over our

things we walked up to the Clarendon Hotel. The {distance}[6]
reported three or four blocks turned out to be nearer twenty.
At last we got to the hotel and found that it had been an old
mansion that had been transformed into a hotel. We got a
lovely room with an old fireplace and a carved plaster ceiling.
After a very nice supper we took a walk down the street. As we
were coming back we found to our surprise that, although it
was broad day-light the real time was after ten. In these regions
in the middle of summer there is hardly any night at all. When
we got back a man came with the trunks and carried them up
to our room on his back. We went to bed full of plans for the
next day. [RJ] {Donnan found a half penny the instant he
touched Ireland. In a drawer in the hotel bedroom, when he
entered.}

DJ June 24, Monday sunny but cold.
Today we got raincoats and boots for all of us. We also went
to see about cars. We found some very nice little cars called
Austin Sevens. They were only 4' 9" high and had seven horse
power but we think we will get a Ford because we know more
about them. The city had been to much for Father and so in
the afternoon he collapsed and lay down on the bed and left
us to our fate. We left Father and went to the bus station to
see if we could go on some interesting trip. We went to Antrim
and had a wounderful time. Father thought it sounded very
interesting and I guess he will go next time. We saw a donkey
lying half underneath a cart today and we thought it must be
dead at least. There were a lot of men busy unharnessing it and
lifted it bodyly to its feet just to fall back again. We thought it
was very cruel but we found it wasn't because the second time
they lifted it trotted happily away. We were passing thrugh the
slumes where there were dirty brick houses and dirtier women
and children when we saw a little thrush in a cage singing
merrily.

---

[6] Added by Una.

DJ June 25, Tuesday sunny but cold Downpatrick—foggy
Father did go with us on our second trip which was to
Downpatrick. There are three Saints buried there St. Patrick
St. Brigid and St. Columb. We saw St. Patrick's grave, a massive
stone uncut except for a cross carved on to it. We could not
find the other two. The Cathedral was very buetiful. There was
a Celtic cross in front of the Cathedral with complicated
interlacing design on it. We went to almost every store in town
and at last got enough food to have a very pleasant lunch
beside a hedge. In Downpatrick there is a German howitzer of
as nearly as we could make out about a nine inch bore. Near
the end of the muzzle there were a number of dents probably
caused by shripnel. Mother took my picture beside it. In
Antrim there is a howitzer of the same type and also an anti-
aircraft machine-gun of about an inch bore. **[GJ]** On the way
back to Belfast two boys with greyhounds got on the bus and
rode into the city. They were probably going to the races.
When we got to Belfast we found that there was still time to
visit the Cathedral Bookstore which mother wanted very much
to do. After getting directions of several policemen we found
ourselves on the right street. We had walked about a block
when we came to the book store. I was going in when I
happened to glance across the street and instantly changed my
mind for over a store were the words "Importer of Foreign
Birds." I went across and looked in the window. In it were
about 20 Shell Paraquets and the same number of Grey Java
Sparrows, the latter were very cheap about 1 shilling apiece.
There were also several finches and one parrot and a big green
paraquet. There were rabbits and guinea pigs and one big
brown animal all curled up in a ball that looked like a cat but a
man near us told father it was a polecat. Inside the shop were
cages and cages of pigeons. **[DJ]** Every day a merry-go-round
goes by our hotel, pulled by two donkeys. It is a small one on
top of a wagon. The benches and horses are brightly colored
and it reminds us of Jackie Yeats' drawings.

[RJ] — —The children of Belfast are more numerous and dirtier than mortal mind can conceive. Crusted skins, ghastly sore eyes and sore noses, poor things. —It was dreadful too to see the terrified drifts of calves and sheep go by to be slaughtered, on the cobbled street between the hard brick walls.

UJ Wednesday, June 26 Temp. is usually about 62° indoors & a bit less outside. We have frozen inside. Can't sit down happily to read or write. —Daylight lasts until 10:30 PM.
[RJ] Started early to Cushendun to find a house. Passed "Ossian's grave." Beautiful country—glens of Antrim—larch plantations all up the steep hillside. Una asked red-faced rich-accented squire in the car what the trees were. "Lorches." Had to walk a mile and a half into Cushendun—lovely bay and shingle— I thought it must be on a lough, the opposite shore so near, but that was Scotland. We walked several miles inquiring cottages to let, but none for July. On the walk back, near Knocknacarry, a man (Alex Martin: who became insane two months later) drew on his leggings by a turf fire and showed us "Dromore Cottage"—very sweet, very little, belongs to a Belfast policeman. We returned to Belfast exhausted, and took the street-cars a long way to the policeman's house, and have got the cottage from his wife for eleven pounds for July and August. [UJ] Went to tiny inn (Mrs. McBride's) for lunch. A photograph of Masefield[7] met our eyes as we entered. He comes there in summer. One darling cottage we might have later but had to cook over coals in fireplace altogether. [RJ] This land looks to me so much younger than ours, though used so long. Its deepest scars are the quarry-pits, each farm has one, but they look natural.
Where we had tea at Cushendun—several green glass globes on the window-sill, (like the one we have at home, the fishing-net float). The woman said they were used to float submarine

[7] John Edward Masefield.

nets during the war, and so many were used that the waves still throw them up the beaches. [DJ] We see lots of donkeys drawing vegtable carts with roses in their harness. [UJ] & forelocks.

DJ Thursday, June 27
This morning we went and bought a Ford car, sedan, 1928 model. Wheels were being painted so we could not have it right away. Mother drove the car of the salesman that helped us buy it and she did very well, it was just the same type. Mother also joined the R.A.C.[8]
[GJ] There is a highland regiment in town and they march by every day in kilts playing the bagpipes. It is very stirring.

RJ Friday June [28] We went by auto-bus to the home village of mother's [Una's] ancestors. The old stone wind-mill towers in the fields, like low round-towers—we saw three on the way to Downpatrick, also. The round-tower seems still to rule the country-people's imagination; their gate-posts, for instance, perfect diminutive round-towers, twinned, at every lane-entrance. (I shall build such in our boundary-fence, when we get home.) The rolling rich green country appeared to Una just like Michigan—if that were chequered with hedge-rows. But here the rock is nearer the plow. [UJ] In churchyard at Killinchy a carved headstone discovered by Donnan leaning over and ivy trailing across said

> "Erected by Robert Henry and John Hamilton of Ballyminstra in memory of John, Elizabeth and Sarah Donnan, who died at an advanced age A.D. 1859."

One part of the church is dated 1759, the other part is dated 1739. Over the 1759 door this carved

> "Keep thy foot when thow goest to
> The House of God & be more ready

---

[8] Royal Automobile Club.

To hear then to give the
Sacrifice of Fools"[9]

[**DJ**] We went to Florada Manner today where great
grandfather Lindsay played as a boy, over 100 years ago. It was
quite a long drive from the lodge with many beautiful verities
of trees beside it. We were going along the drive when all of a
sudden, rounding a bend, we came upon the manner. It was
beautiful old building though quite delapadated. It was three
stories high besides a large cellar which we could see through
gratings in the stone pavement that surrounded the house. The
mane house was about square with one wing jutting of to the
right and one to the rear. Mother took two pictures of it which
were all she had left. We were sitting outside on the lawn
looking at it when a woman came out. Mother opened a
conversation with her and she invited us in. The front rooms
were not used and they were not furnished. The entrance hall
entered into a large hall which in turn entered into a library and
dinning room as far as we could make out. [**GJ**] We were
looking around when I saw several white Orpingtons which of
course attracted me to the spot. I looked around a low shed
and saw the first game bantam I had ever seen. It was of the
old fashioned fighting type and was a kind of silver, laced with
black and brown. It was stalking very dignifiedly across the
yard when I gave a soft crow. It immediatly gave a sharp cackle
and I, fearing that it would alarm the house, immediatly
withdrew. I was rounding an out building when I caught the
clink of a chain inside, I looked in and made out the form of
an immense shorthorn bull. Mother took one glance in and
immediatly began edging away. After a while we went and sat
under an immense evergreen and admired the manor. Pretty
soon we heard the beat of hooves and saw a man leading a
huge Clydesdale mare with a little colt by her side. The man
stopped and talked to us about the colt, it was only two days

---

[9] Ecclesiastes 5:1.

old but it was frisking all over and was bigger than a lot of
Shetland ponies that I have seen. Pretty soon another man
came up with a draft horse in harness and called to the man to
lead the colt on. [UJ] I asked the man whether there were any
walks paved or strewn with shells in the grounds. Grandfather
had talked of them. He said the driveway which swept so
proudly in the old days up to the portico had many broken
shells in it (just below the surface now). It was all very beautiful
the bright sunshine and great trees and the gray old house so
dignified even now. Before we went to Florida Manor we
called at *The Craigs* where 17 years ago I had called upon our
connections Mrs. Hewitt & Miss Wilson.[10] A Mrs. Thomas
Robinson lives there & when I went in & explained us, she was
most cordial and talked a great deal about the country around
& then after we had walked around the yard she asked us to
come in again. She had prepared a little lunch for us because
she feared we could not get any in Killinchy. Tea & bread &
soda bread & potato bread & sweet cakes & jam. A lovely
garden & roses everywhere. —Afterwards we called at a quaint
clean rose-bedecked farm of Mrs. Auld, born a Donnan. She
was very shy but finally talked to us. We could not trace our
relationship if any. I promised to return another day after she
had made inquiries of relatives. Gigantic geese hissed at us
here.

UJ Saturday June 29—
  [DJ] Mother completed her arrangements with the R.A.C. She
also got her driving license. On the way home we stopped at a
shop. Father looked so bored that we let him go on. Mother
bought a beutiful bog-oak carved walking stick but just as we
were going out, Garth noticed a crack right where the handle
joins the stick so mother made them take it back. When we got
back to the hotel we found that our car had come. Mother did
not think we would need it so she told the man to take it back

---

[10] Mary (Wilson) Hewitt and her sister Jane Wilson.

to the garage till Monday. In the afternoon we went to the bookstore. Father and Mother could not find any interesting books but Garth got stuck on a natural history in three huge volumes that weighed about a ton. Mother finaly tore him away with great sorrow on his part.

DJ Sunday June 30

In the morning mother packed. At 3:30 we got on the train for Marino where Mr. Praeger's sister and mother live. We had never been in a European train before and thought it very strange. The train stoped and we got out and asked the guard whether it was Marino. He said "Yes." Miss Praeger had promised to meet us but hunt as we would we could not finde her. At last we found it Holywood and not Marino. We were in despair but at last we discovered an ancient pre-war taxi with a very cross driver. When we got there we had tea. Although Mrs. Praeger is 90 years old she looked very well. Some friends of theirs came namely Mr. and Mrs. Neil. They took us down to the harbor of the Yacht Club. There were several yachts drawn up on the beach.

DJ Monday, July 1 fair

[**GJ**] Got up early and finished packing. When our car came the man drove us down to Cooks where Mother finished paying him for the car. Then mother went and got an oil stove and I got the natural history books. At about ten we started off and had a lunch of cookies and chocolate. At Cushendall we went threw a fair. We got out and walked over to a cart to look at some pigs. Mrs. Evans was still at the cottage and showed mother different things about the management of the place. Alex Martin told us about some of his experiences with ferrets. On the way through Carrick Fergus we saw the Castle. We got out and walked around it for a while. When we looked at the walls we thought it looked impossible to scale them even in peace time.

UJ Tues, July 2 Unpacked, settled in and late in the day drove down to Cushendun. Had dealings in eggs, butter, milk & poultry & turf with a dear old Irish neighbor woman Mrs. McKillop. Boys rejoice in numerous farm animals.

UJ Wed July 3 drove to Ballycastle & Giant's Causeway also to Dunluce Castle & to Carrick-a-rede Bridge. {On way to Ballycastle a little fairy lake, Loughareema, which vanishes mysteriously in summer—lies in midst of wild high moors.} Drove over the mountain where all the ~~peat~~ turf is cut. Its a five mile haul to Knocknacarry. Picked a bunch of bog cotton. Drove under & over the spectacular Glendun Viaduct. {Bought Irish whisky at Bushmills very expensive. 7/6[11] for less than pint}

UJ [Thursday] July 4. Garth ill high temp. Has gotten an intestinal infection vomiting & diarrhea probably from old buttermilk we drank. Hunted up a doctor. None nearer than Cushendall. He came Dr. O Kane—didn't trust him much at first—he was a whole degree off in taking temp. but he proved sensible. Garth's fever went on all night. **[DJ]** Did the routine things. **[UJ]** This was the 4th of July. Scared to have boys ill over here! Doctor 15/

UJ [Friday] July 5. Garth gets better today. O Kane again this morn (10/ this time) Garth has a very red face & red eyes. Dr would think coming down with measles if he hadn't had them, still on liquid diet. Temp becomes normal. Enjoy turf fire. Manage cooking better than I would have thought possible over open fire & little oil stove. Cooked a chicken over turf fire, delicious —Turf smoke fragrant. —a bit like oak. Hard to get used to daylight lasting all night! Neighbors drop in to chat at 11 P.M.

---

[11] Until 1971 the British Isles used the pound ($£1$), shilling (1/), pence (pennies) monetary system. 7/6 is 7 shillings, 6 pence. A lower case d often follows the number of pence.

Seem never to go to bed. Country very beautiful. Hedges &
green rolling country & streams & stone bridges & walls.
Hedges of pink & white may, pink & white briar roses, yellow
& pink honeysuckle & blackberries. This little cabin is a priest's
house wrecked in the "trouble" & repaired. 4 rooms (2
bedrooms, living room & kitchen (& coal & turf lean to & privy
lean-to) house very clean. Some fine old pieces of furniture,
mahogany tilt-top table, black walnut dresser & cherry (little)
table with leaves, some good pieces of china 2 precious
Lustreware pitchers. Didn't know so primitive a countryside
existed in Northern Ireland racy dialect very friendly &
amusing people, wish I could write down their idioms. Mrs.
McK says when she goes outside to feed the animals all the
house "goes astray." Said of people who jumped off high
bridge— They were "away in their ~~minds~~ heads." Darling little
Peter (Payter) McK. said when boys told him of their long
holiday in summer "and sure thats a long halt." —He comes
to the door & says, "And how are the wee fellows the day?"

DJ [Saturday] July 6 Garth is getting beter. I visited the McKillops.
They were very friendly. Mr. McK. told me to come up every
day and they would let me ride their pony.

DJ [Sunday] July 7 Father and Mother thought Garth was well
enough to take a trip. We went along the coast road, thrugh
Waterfoot to Glenarm and then across to Ballymena, then to
Cushendall, and home. Garth got rather tired on the trip and
had a slight set-back.

DJ [Monday] July 8— Mother went to Cushendall today to do
some shopping. She made many blunders such as when she
wanted motor spirits she asked for gasoline, when she wanted
essence of rennet she asked for junket tablets, when she
wanted corn flour and rice corns she asked for corn starch and
plane rice and so on.

UJ [Tuesday] July 9 —Father sick. Garth's complaint. Dreary day. Mother & Donnan walk to Knocknacarry P. O.

UJ [Wednesday] July 10— Drove to Ballycastle. There to Fair Head. Wild remote place. **[DJ]** Walked in the rain a mile across a wild moor to the edge of the cliff. 650 feet down we could see sheep grazing in a small field between the botom and the sea. **[UJ]** Most vivid and lovely rainbow we ever saw. {Lambs & sheep bleating on the misty moorland.} **[DJ]** {Within a little glen near the summit of Fair Head are two small loughs, called Loch Dubh and Loch-na-Cranagh—this the Black Lake and the Lake of Crannog or Artificial Island. The Island is prehistorick.} Went to Ballycastle to do some shopping. It was a half holiday and so we couldn't buy anything.

UJ Thurs July. 11   Rain. Drove to Layde Graveyard, through Cushendall. Got off trail and walked mile through wet meadow & tall grass. Fine old ruins. Many curious old tombstones with strange devices, and the arms of the McDonnell family —& the motto written variously Semper paratus, Tout jour prêt, Sword in Hand. Fine old holed stone interested us near stile. In one old chapel many tombs of McAulays. —Copied some epitaphs. Isn't this one pitiful—

> **[GJ]** Here lieth the body of John Hyndman who departed this life shortly after his return from Buenos Ayres on the 29th of July 1830 aged 33 years.

[UJ] Layde is backed by forest trees & falls off steeply to wild sea. Mts not far away. Ossian's Grave up a soaking lane to top of a lonely hill a kind of stone circle.

UJ Friday Orange Day July 12 Started on travels. Lovely weather Cushendun, Orange Day celebrations. In Free State were straggling bands of Orangemen very enthusiastically drilling in the lanes and feeling very daring. **[GJ]** We think the Free State looks very prosperous along here: A few straggling bands of

Orangmen in the Free State: little gardens full of bright flowers, bright paint around windows. Wild dash to get across the border before five and we only managed it by courtesy of customs man at Monaghan. Stopped at sunset at the strange old town of Clones and saw a round tower and many tombstones, alot of which had skulls and crossbones on them, dinner at Cavan and then went on to the Greville Arms at Granard. It is a very queer "out of the world" town and now no one visits it apparently. When Mother asked for Athlone in the morning no one knew where Athlone was although it was the biggest town in the vicinity and was but 35 miles away. The round tower at Clones was made of rough stones not shaped. Our trip was via these ~~big~~ towns: [UJ] about 650 miles

underline where all night
^{X} where dinner
^{O} Round Tower

Knocknacarry, Parkmore, Ballymena, Antrim, Moira, Lurgan, Portadown, Armagh, Monaghan, Clones^O, Cavan^X, Granard, Edgeworthtown, Ballymahon, Athlone, Clonmacnoise^{OO}, Shannonbridge, Ballinsloe, Loughrea, Gort, (Yeats' Ballylee), Kiltartan, Edward Martyn's Tillyra, Oranmore, Galway, Oughterard, Maam Cross, Recess, Clifden, Letterfrack, Leeane, Glenane, Westport, Castlebar^X, Lough Carra, George Moore's Moore Hall, Ballinrobe, Claremorris, Ballyhaunis, Castlerea, Frenchpark, Carrick on Shannon, Ballinamore, Swanlinbar (spa), Enniskillen (Devenish Island^O on Lough Erne), Omagh, Carrickamore, Cookstown, Tobermore, Maghera, Kilrea, Rasharkin, Ballymoney, Armoy^O, Aura Rd, Cushendall, Knocknacarry.

UJ Saturday—July 13   Sunny. Went through Edgeworthtown thought of Walter Scott visiting Maria Edgeworth there — Robin asked native about Maria—no intelligence—finally said "Yes, there was a Miss E—" Robin said "about a hundred years ago." Ans= "No she isn't quite as old as that. Her sister got married lately." Reached the seven churches of Clonmacnoise about 1 PM. Very hot. —there in that remote

spot a blue lake-like stretch of the Shannon with one little
house in the distance, reeds at edge of water, then meadows
and men cutting hay, then up a slope—and a beautiful round
tower minus its top—up against it a wall, then the churchyard
—a beautiful Celtic cross— old old tombs—ruins of several
churches then down the slope a part of another chapel & at its
side a little round tower, —we sat very quietly in the hot haze
and gazed about us. I shall never forget this place such quiet.
One of the finest ruins in Ireland. {The ancient Irish university.
In one shrine a queer pile of offerings, pennies, buttons, bent
pins, etc. Little fields of blue flax are lovely.} I should have said
at Athlone our first country fair, mostly pigs & chickens, —
women with shawls over head everywhere. Great dirt. At
Ballinasloe sent cards to Adele and Mrs. Overstreet from their
mother's birthplace.[12] Arrived at Gort. Old hotel & friendly
host (with wine shop at corner). He said "*Old* (shocked me)
Mr. Yeats[13] passed here not ten minutes ago on way to see Lady
Gregory at Coole Park." We ordered dinner. It was just 8 PM.
Said it would be at least half hour preparing so we could go to
Ballylee Castle Yeats' tower. —It was 4 miles opposite way
from Coole. —Stoney country rolling country thorn trees &
windy bushes a few goats on the hills—bare country, some
peat cut. We saw it at last & turned into a lane —there it stood
by a little winding stream all as we had foreseen. —the quiet
austere strong square tower with the tiny houses at its feet
several of them all attached to each other some slate roof
some thatch a walled garden in rear —all the windows boarded
up tight—with green shutters. One strange head set into wall
of tower about 15 ft up above ground, an Egyptian cast of face
—a stone arched bridge narrow adjoins house —a peasant was
watering her cows there —then another came with a wooden
tub on a donkey cart—to fill the tub with water —this carrying

---

[12] Adele (Fortier) Bechdolt and her sister Kathryn (Fortier) Overstreet.
Their mother, Anna Freer, was born in Ireland.
[13] William Butler Yeats.

water an incredible ordeal all over Ireland. She said Mrs. Yeats
& the children were there last year but not Mr. Y— He was
sick. On the stone wall "Mary Hynes" —and some other words
written in red chalk. A little garth across the lane was sweet
with new-mown hay. This tower is very solitary. No suave &
spacious estates & manors near —not even little farm houses.
The sun began to set —it was very quiet and solitary. My heart
beat very hard!

DJ Sunday [July 14]

Stayed over night at Lally's Royal Hotel, Gort. Had a nice
night. We went through Kiltartan (and thought of Lady
Gregory) to Edward Martyns Tillyra. **[UJ]** We asked at the
lodge gate if we might drive in —the gate man said "Yes, Mr—
had just gone in to follow him" —The night before in the
street I had talked long with a quaint old person who was some
sort of town official. He said he had once had the great honor
of introducing Edward Martyn & Arthur Griffiths! He talked
of Martyn— he left his estate to his nephew— but he hasn't
money enough to keep it up properly & its going to ruin. He
talked of Lady Gregory & Yeats—Yeats' spiritualism— (I
think he referred to *seances*) very deep in it now— —. We drove
[DJ] {Then we went to Galway and saw the Lynch House and
the window out of which the Chief Magistrate Lynch hung his
own son in 1495— **[UJ]** his son had killed a guest a Spaniard—
a terrible story. My breath caught as I stood there—}[14] a mile
past the gates—beautiful park—great trees oak & ash & maple
& beech, etc — — Came in sight of the old (1400) and new
(1882) castles joined together & around an enormous stone
paved courtyard. The owner had just gotten out of his car. {Dr.
Oliver Gogarty of Dublin at Tor House said this present owner
of Tillyra is Lord Hemphill[15]} I explained our interest in E. M.
and he was very charming (reminded me of John O'Shea). He

---

[14] A circle is drawn around this insertion, setting it off from the main text.
[15] Martyn Charles Andrew Hemphill, 4th Baron Hemphill.

said he hadn't had breakfast but if we cared to walk about the grounds for a bit, as soon as he had eaten he would take us up into the tower—(a big square one, 14 cent —like Yeats' only very *large*). —We went out through arched gate into gardens and walked about. {Ate great red raspberries off bushes.} — The place would need a hundred servants to keep it up —it looked neglected & run down. —We talked about the architecture of the place & George Moores description of it all & E. M. —I wonder does anyone know that all as well as I — At last the great front doors undid with great clangor & Mr— asked us to come in. How strange as we went in to see these pillars of black marble Arthur Symons talks about—in the hall —The great pipe organ on which E. M. played Palestrina is gone (sold—said the nephew) —Almost plaintively he spoke of E. M. endowing the great Palestrina Choir in Dublin (lots of money went into that!) He showed us a few rooms great library & dining room (servants just clearing the great table.) —A beautiful very fair young woman of sweet dignity—his wife made us welcome —showed us some family portraits on walls —showed us great room used by E. M. as billiard room—now a sitting room —showed us magnificent great Spanish fireplace *old* (mantel) of grey marble (in library) taken from E. M.'s castle at Kinvarra. {Mantel now returned to Kinvarra Castle now owned by Dermot Gogarty (son of Oliver)} How *thick* with memories all those rooms for me— —then up the stairs in the thickness of wall of the tower to E. M.s oratory & study. We saw various hiding places & cubby holes & strong room (with a mass of papers foot thick lying on floor in confusion) —his bedroom etc all dismantled just stray pieces of furniture. Up, up to top of tower & around the battlements warned us to step lightly on boards laid down so nails would not penetrate the leads. This man seemed almost desperate to me in his longing to keep the place up as it should be & the *burden* of it —the taxes must be overwhelming. He was both proud and apologetic— — {He pointed out a high elm, said to be one of the highest trees in Ireland —a splendid wood—great ash &

maple & beech & oak} —They said we were free to wander
about as much as we wished but we were on our way to
Connemara so we had to go—

The women now begin to be seen with the fawn colored shawls
—a few red petticoats. I miss the donkeys with panniers—
Connemara is beautiful but not as much so as I remembered it
—Great space—and fine mts. & lakes & streams.

One fine castle Kylemore —much turf cut —heather darker
than in Antrim. Strange to meet girls on bicycles & on foot
very much dressed up—silk stockings etc Get to Castlebar for
dinner. —There I begin to inquire how to get to Moore Hall.
Found 3 old men who gave directions —didn't agree very well
—Then a wild fellow very drunk began to talk —he seemed
very familiar with Moore Hall. We decided from his excitement
& assurance that he had been a dependent there. He insisted I
take an altogether other road by Claremorris —We started
about 7:30 from Castlebar —still some time before sunset but
after many inquiries & slow motion as we were in a lonely road
we had a blow-out. I felt desperate. —R began to change tire
when a big bus passed us —Then over a rise of ground & we
heard screeching of brakes & wild gabble of voices —boys ran
back & found the bus had hit an old woman's cow. Fearful din
& excitement —Went on asked again & again—one turn after
another —Country more & more wild —at last the gates of
Moore Hall—*locked*. We drove a few rods to gate house and a
very pretty intelligent girl came out & gave us the key when we
told her who we were. We drove along the dim avenue under
enormous trees—at last the house & a surge of emotion *in me*.
It rose 3 stories—square gengian gray stone with fine pillared
portico—iron railed balcony above it. It is a shell only—the
entire interior gutted with fire in the "Troubles." Outside much
covered with ivy. We went inside & gazed at the noble
proportions of the hall & lower rooms. Looked out in rear at
walled garden & forest beyond. Looked down into many
vaulted cellars. —Then in front from the steps where Geo
Moore in his letter to me had pictured himself waiting to

receive me —There swept away one of the sweetest vistas I have ever seen from any house— (Memo Over portico on stone is carved

> 1795
>
> Fortis cadere N O N (like this)
>   cedere
> non potest."[16])

Directly in front of the house there were no trees, although at both sides the forest was thick and high. —from the house the ground slopes steadily and gently down about 250 yds to a sweet lake Lough Carra —half way down on a level bit, is a sundial. There are tiny islands in the lake covered with trees. On one we saw a small tower—probably the Castle Carra Moore speaks of where he and the other children often went with their nurse to picnic. I have never seen a finer situation for a house. —As we walked about the red sunset glow died through the trees behind the house —a lone bird—we thought a whip-poor-will sang plaintively in the forest. I picked a spray of very fragrant white flowers from a bush —Fragrant like syringa—only more sweet. We took a fragment of stone to build into Tor House. I just adored this visit. —We returned the key and the pleasant girl said Col Maurice Moore had just visited Moore Hall & talked of restoring it. George M. had not been there for a long time. I told her we had been to Edward Martyn's Tillyra Castle & she was interested & said "Mr. Martyn was a great friend of Mr. George Moore." When we thanked her she always said "Thanks for nothing." She told us a better way out of the maze of roads & lanes to Ballinrobe, where we spent the night in a miserable hotel. Horrid breakfast. Left in a temper at overcharge & hungry. Our usual lunch on our trip was cheese & crackers or biscuits, oranges & cakes. Our first day we had tea in thermos from home.

---

[16] "The brave may fall, but never yield."

Afterwards bought a bottle of lemon & lime juice & had lemonade. We always finished with bars of chocolate.

UJ Monday— [July 15] A fair at Claremorris where I saw the pig market 17 years ago. [**GJ**] When we drove into Claremorris we found that a fair was going on, just as there was when Mother was there before we were born. All along this beginning of the main street were the sheep, hundreds and hundreds of them, all hobbled. Farther up were horses, most of them heavy draft horses, Clydesdales and Shires. We had to get a tire fixed and so while it was being mended I and Donnan took a stroll back up an alley-way, where we came across alot of donkeys for sale. There were a lot of eggs lying on the street and we concluded that there had been a chicken sale earlier in the morning. Just as we started up a truckload of pigs arrived and men began hauling them around by the ears to the accompaniment of terrific squeals. When we got to the outskirts of the town we came to the cattle part of the fair, several thousand head milling around with men haggling at the outskirts of the herd.
[**UJ**] Robin says the only thing that exceeds the intensity of the women's eyes here is the limp vacancy of the men's.
Think the green-blue spray used everywhere on potatoes, & colouring the sprayer & his clothes & cart so vividly as characteristic as the reddleman of Hardy.[17] Two great activities all along the way. Cutting turf —then haying. All along the 2 wheeled red wagons carrying home turf.
People always sitting in groups or alone idly in hedges.
On a lonely road we passed a straggling little company carrying a coffin shoulder-high. Arrived at Enniskillen a fine looking town built high above the beautiful waters of Lough Erne. Old Enniskillen Castle with 2 beautiful round turrets at edge of lake. We got a man to take us in his motor boat out to Devenish Island (about 2 miles) to see the Round Tower & church ruin. A fine tower, top & all intact with a fragment of

---

[17] Thomas Hardy.

dear little church above. A tiny stair in thickness of wall—a magnificent Celtic cross. [**DJ**] The round tower had two grotesque heads carved out of stone near the top. The man said that scientists and antiquaries had come from all over the world to see them. No other round tower has them. In the ruined monistery there was an old stone coffin without a top or bottom. It was about this shape: It is called a wishing coffin in which people lie and make a wish. There were a great many swans on the lake. The shores were very thickly covered with reeds, and it was very hard to get the boat in. We went back and went to the best hotel in town to see if we could get a decent meal. The answer was the inveribel one, that they could give us cold meat and tea. Mother said that that was what she had had for almost a weak and made such a row that they said we could have dinner. It was very good. Drove on to a fine hotel in Omagh for the night. [**UJ**] {Omagh is a finely piled up town of gray stone with steeples—} [**DJ**] I should of {have}[18] mentioned that there was a stairs going to the door of the round tower at Devenish Island and a goat used to go up and keep people from going up. [**UJ**] They used to have to bring an oar from the boat to fight him off. {At the custom station the officer took us to drink sulphur water at the spa. (Swanlinbar Station)}

DJ Tuesday July 16 Royal Hotel Omagh.
There was a loud thunder storm this morning about six. It sounded like all the slate of the roof falling down on us. A little fox-terrier dog excaped out of a window and ran out on to [**UJ**] {the edge of the} [**DJ**] roof of a neighboring house. We felt sure it was going to fall off. [**UJ**] Across the roofs was a clock and it was flanked by a great carved stone lion & unicorn. We came home by Armoy to see the round tower—a stump about 30 ft high in a churchyard. Quiet & far removed from turmoil. Ivy on it. Adjoining was a country vicarage— men mowing

---

[18] Added by Una.

hay. A dead raven somehow was affixed to the tower near top. We got inside this tower. We came home over Aura Mt to Cushendall. A fine mt road little frequented. Scenery as fine as Connemara. Wide sweep mts finely lined up gloomy and grand. We got out and sat on the heather. Never a soul in sight— but sheep bleating on the hills— lonely cry of curlews and the sound of ever falling water. Got home. Wire from Ellen visit postponed. Wire from Percy— wants to come but is ill, has insomnia.[19]

UJ Wed July 17 Rested & cleaned up. Donnan not well   stayed in bed part of day.

UJ Thurs July [18] Went to Ballycastle. Rained. Got 3 boys hairs cut. Finally found lamp shade to take place of one Donnan broke.

UJ Friday July [19]— Managing food better. Cooked a chicken over turf fire. Found better supplies. Washed hair. *Silky*— rain water did it. Boys went to school with Peter. The master pressed boys to tell of their travels and of California. Children had thought oranges grew wild & luxuriant all over California. Wild drunken man from Cushenlik stamped & shouted a long time here in the road. Sang and flourished a knife & said he was the bravest man in the Glens of Antrim.

UJ Saturday, July [20] Wrote letters. Lovely day. Made plans for next trip. Beggar woman to door. I, sitting there writing, said, "Go away. You are the third in five minutes." She turned from me in a frenzy and began to rave and swish her skirt—a fine histrionic frenzy. "So it's you, Biddy Moriarty, a-striding before me taking the bit bread from my mouth, and me to let you sleep in my byre, and you to say, Stand aside, Mary, and

---

[19] Ellen O'Sullivan, a friend from Carmel traveling in Europe. Percy Peacock, an English friend of Una's.

a-pulling away your skirt!" And off she went talking on with me entirely forgotten.

RJ Sunday, July [21]. I wrote a few lines of doubtful verse yesterday and to-day, for the first time since the "Shepherdess." We start to-day on a new pilgrimage. It was raining so much that we did not visit Florida Manor again, as we meant to, but started late from ~~home~~ Knocknacarry, gazed at the Antrim round tower from the road through a veil of trees—"for two years the public have not been admitted"—and reached Belfast and the Clarendon Hotel in time to have supper about seven. The same nice big room is assigned us. After supper we drove to [UJ] Newtownards, Donaghadee (& thought of Hardy's verse) and back—via Bangor and Holywood through showers. —Caught a glimpse of Helen's Tower at Clandeboye through trees on the height. Bangor crowded—bands and banners— Boys in boisterous spirits.

RJ Monday, July [22]. We spent the night at the Clarendon, and the morning in having the car (Emily IV!)[20] thoroughly lubricated, and having our papers changed at the R.A.C. to permit a sixth tyre (which we bought) to cross the border with us. Before noon we drifted out, however, and went prosperously to Armagh, where we drove about to see the Navan Fort—Emain Macha—where grew ~~lovely~~ honey-smelling clustered delicate flowers on the old earth-works, and a gnarled ring of thorn-trees about the central mound. Very solitary, except a few children tossing hay in a field below. Garth found two badgers' burrows in the earth-works. From there to the customs station on the border we lost our way a very little and came by surprise on an old Gaelic cross at a turn of the road in a village on a hill called Tynan—a wonderful old cross with four bosses on the four arms. [UJ] Saw again the Round tower at Clones, spent night at Boyle where there is a

---

[20] The Jefferses called all their cars "Emily."

marvellous ruined abbey "important ruins" said guidebook
founded in the 11 century. —Softly gurgling river ran under
our windows at hotel and then through stone arched bridge.
Looking out in the other direction long line of old stone houses
with their walls washed by the river. Brilliant moonlight.
Looked out in night upon a beautiful scene. River bridge
houses and splashing water. —Trout for breakfast!

UJ Tuesday July [23] Next day on toward Achill. —Bare, bleak,
meager peasants, miserable & wretched lives. Stayed at Achill
Hotel, horrid accommodation and intolerable food. In evening
walked to old Dugort and on to next hamlet, saw funny goose
fall on his nose in getting over wall, then rise up and strut with
head thrown back—leading his flock. We laughed very hard—
boys offered us amethyst stones found there, —talked with
lame old man, told us of death of Henri the painter just now
in America who lives in Capt Boycott's house.[21] Don't like
Achill—dreadful lives the people live— they seem thin &
vague and suspicious. I got out of car to take picture of little
ass carrying 2 pannier baskets loaded with turf accompanied by
baby ass. —Old terrible woman rushed out aggressively
scolding me. —She didn't seem to want me to take picture.
Compromised by making me take one of her daughter & son
& agree to send to her. Daughter very sulky, kept saying
something. At last made me promise not to "distribute"
pictures of her.

> This trip consumed 760 miles and went thus: Knocknacarry,
> Cushendall, Ballymena, Antrim[O], Belfast, (Newtownards,
> Donaghadee, Bangor, Holywood, Belfast) Lisburn, Lurgan,
> Portadown, Armagh, Middletown, Monaghan, Clones[O],
> Belturbet, Ballinamore[X], Fenagh, Carrick-on-Shannon, Boyle,
> Gorteen, Tobercurry, Ballina, Crossmolina, Bangor, Ballycroy,
> Mallaranny, Achill, Doogart[X], Achill, Mallaranny, Newport,

---

[21] Robert Henri, American artist who died July 12, 1929; Charles
Cunningham Boycott, an English land agent.

Castlebar, Turlough°, Swinford, Melick°, Ballymote, Collooney, Sligo^X, Drumcliffe°, Bundoran, Ballyshannon, <u>Donegal</u>, Killybegs, Carrick, Glencolumbkille, Ardara, Glenties, Ballybofey, Lifford, Strabane^X, <u>Londonderry</u>, Limavady, Coleraine, Portrush, Bushmills, Ballycastle, Cushendun, Knocknacarry

Lots of red petticoats here—sometimes whole red dress makes nice splotch of color. Roads very bad, narrow & full of sharp stones, ruination to tires. —On the way here just before we got to Ballina we saw a perfectly formed rath or tumulus (mound) in middle of hollow plain. Presently saw a peasant cutting turf asked him he said the place was called *See* Finn. The old people thought it was built by former inhabitants. Met at hotel a Dublin woman friend of Ella Young and Ernie O'Malley. She knew Gaelic. Said words meant *Seat* of Finn. Saw old castle on distant hills—square with corner towers, well spread out— looked *Italian*—Castle of Dermot McDermot.

UJ Wed. July [24] Gladly departed from Achill. Geese have been everywhere through Ireland. We speak too of the hedgers— people always sitting on or by the hedges—all along the way— [DJ] We saw three round towers today, all of which were unexpected. In Castlebar Mother saw a poscard of a round tower and a church called Turlough Tower. She made inquiries and found it was on our road to the next town. It was a very good one. It was quite a small one with its top on. It was built right up against the church. The next one was Melick. Garth saw it first on a distant hill. After going by winding lanes and byroads we got to it. It was the tallest one we have yet seen allthough its roof was lacking. Father pointed out that the four windows were gone at the top so it must have been at least fifteen feet higher. The third one was right outside Sligo about 8 miles. It was right beside the road. It was just a stump about 30 feet high. Its name was Drumcliffe. There were alot of trees around it and between some of them that were specially close together there were big wads of straw and grass. We could not immagin what they were for and we asked a man that came along. He said that cows sometimes got stuck between them and could not get out. Across the road was a church and a graveyard in which was a Celtic cross. We asked the man about it and he said that there used to be 14 of them besides a plain one which was still standing but had no head. Father said it looked like the oldest stone in the world. In a field near the church there was a milk white kid goat that Garth thought looked like a unicorn. [GJ] We have been surprised at the number of swans, wild and tame, all over Ireland. In almost every lake that we passed there have been two or more swans. At Sligo as we were going away after supper Donnan happened to look over a bridge and said that there were at least a hundred swans swimming around in the water below us. Mother stopped the car and we got out and looked over the edge in the water. Swimming around were the most swans that we have ever seen before together. Father counted thirty-six but it looked like twice as many. [UJ] By the stone bridge where the swans were congregated was a weir and the water splashed white by the white of the swans and a few sea gulls were white above them. In Sligo is a very fine old abbey ruin with beautiful doors and windows date 1252. Excellent dinner at Great Southern Railway Hotel. Fine drive through sunshiny evening along coast. —We meditated turning to Rosses Point hoping to see Jack Yeats' *Iron Man* in the harbour —but drove on. We often thought of Wm Butler Yeats as we went through his own country and through Colooney (near Coolaney) with its bits of blue lake water and whispering reeds. Saw name *Pollexfen* (Yeats's mother's family) over big building in Sligo. Beautiful country here. —Stopped at Donegal for night. Had a look at ruins of Donegal Castle near hotel on the river —finest ruins yet seen and interesting walk through town to old abbey ruins bordering the river. —A big black hooker moored to grassy landing near abbey ruins held us for a bit. In this abbey was written the *Annals of the 4 Masters*. In morning fine trout for breakfast. Again to Castle with the custodian. Marvellous carved fireplace & much carving over windows & doors. A thrilling square turret at one end. —

A joke that in George Moore's *Castlebar* village I bought a copy of Hardy's *"Under the Greenwood Tree."*[22] Forgot to say at Achill old man told us of dreadful winter weather —last year the ~~peat~~ turf did not dry properly & got mouldy and then froze and when they pried the chunks apart and put them on the fire out oozed steam—but no heat! Clouds very beautiful here. Between Sligo & Donegal very fine sheer ramparted hills & cliffs in sharp jagged outline.

UJ Thurs. July [25] Drove to Killybegs and Kilcar & by bad road to Glencolumbkille supposed to be favorite spot of St. Columb and filled with antiquities. It is Donegals farthest west village. Villagers were reluctant to give information. One horrible filthy half drunken beggar pestered us to take him on as guide. Saw three old stones with pre-Christian markings. As we were leaving (my thoughts on the wretched stone-filled road up the hill we had to negotiate) an old man with a cow talked to us of some relics on the shore and of smuggling here in the old days and of an underground chapel which some man came 17 yrs. ago and cleaned out and had helpers & they worked a fortnight at it and the man was drowned soon after and no one knows who he was or who sent him and now the chapel is full of filth again. Near Killybegs is a sacred well to which there are frequent pilgrimages. All down the center of village street were booths which sold exclusively relics, amulets, sacred images & pictures scapulars & holy fonts. Vistas of Donegal Highlands all day. Grand and gloomy scenery. Night at Londonderry. Walk around walls of fine old town. Saw different bastions now flower gardens. Saw ~~Hanging~~ *Hangman's Bastion*. Saw old cannon "Roaring Meg"—— saw tall monument of the parson who in 16— led the defenders of the city successfully.

---

[22] In his 1971 transcription of the diary, Donnan inserted "(Moore hated Hardy.)" here.

UJ Friday July 26 Home today. Stopped to shop in Portrush, clean enterprising town near Giant's Causeway. Saw good things to eat (not often in Ireland) home about 3. —Went to Knocknacarry P. O. Found great batch of letters and Postmistress excited about various telegrams waiting us. — Percy Peacock had arrived in Larne night before and was waiting our arrival in Cushendall. Went & found him and brought him to hotel at Cushendun after tea in Dromore Cottage. He isnt much changed only face is fatter, not so sensitive, he looks very prosperous—no lines in his face—hair gray but he looks younger than when I saw him last in 1913. Acted constrained at first.

UJ Sat. July 27 Took Percy to Armoy Round Tower via Ballycastle then back over Aura Mountain. Took our tea along and stopped overlooking wild glen to eat & drink. He was really surprised at the wide & gloomy horizon— Rain at intervals.

UJ Sunday July 28 Percy at Dromore Cottage. —Stayed for dinner— I cooked a chicken over turf fire. Also— peas & new potatoes. Had some good port. Rain almost all day.

UJ Monday July 29 Lunch (boys & I) with Percy at Cushendun. Afterwards sat on sand. Boys threw endless stones into water and P & I talked about our lives & looked across the sea to Scotland. Back here for tea— then we drove to Ballymena & back by coast home. Rain.

UJ Tuesday July 30 Percy & I went to Catholic churchyard and found a few old tomb stones— then we drove under Glendun Viaduct. Rain. Rain. Percy to tea here at Dromore Cottage, then we drove him to Larne (29 miles) to take the evening boat to Scotland. Lovely ride back. Thunderous clouds & showers of rain with intervals of brilliant sunshine.

The brilliant blue green of the potato spraying and the blue green cans are as characteristic and full of color as Hardy's reddleman.

On our last trip we noticed on scattered cottages (on the thatched roofs) bits of bright red rags tied to little sticks and thrust into thatch. Couldn't imagine why unless to scare away evil spirits (like red rag in bowl of Grandmother Donnan's lamp).

UJ Wednesday, July 31. Rain. Rain. Rain. Rested today. [**DJ**] A tramp came to the door today and wanted a sixpence. Mother said that there was a constant stream of them comming to the door all the time and she was fed up with it. He said he was fed up with wanting a drink, and Mother shut the door in his face. Father finished "Under the Greenwood Tree." It is a very merry rustic little story that hasn't a sorroful ending like most of Hardy.

DJ Thursday, August 1 Very windy but hot. Temp 3 P.M. 82° Temp 8 P.M. 54°.

Took a long walk about 7 miles. We went first to Cushendun and then to the Pratistent church on Lord Cushendun's estate to see a ruin which Percy thought was a round tower. We could not find it so we walked on along the beach and saw a tower old and almost covered with ivy. Father thought it was a castle that the guide book spoke of. We were throwing stones into the water, and Father and Mother were a little ways ahead when Mother saw a stone fall into the water several hundred feet out. She couldnt believe her eyes but in a few seconds a bird came up and flew away. We noticed several of them. They flew around about a hundred feet above the water and then dropped like a plumit making a great splash and disappering completly. [**UJ**] We walked on to Shane O'Neil's cairn in a high field beside the hilly cliff road to Ballycastle. It is a huge round pile of stones —for centuries tradition has said that the body of S. O'N lies there. Set into the pile of stones near the top are several cut stones with carvings on. One says Shane O'Neil 1567—and a hand (red hand of Ulster?) the other stones have recent dates on like 1897—or 1902 and the names of Shane Leslie (enthusiasts) etc with Celtic interlaced patterns one the Hebridean laced design with snakes' heads. —We walked back. —By the stone (Episcopal) Church on Lord Cushendun's estate is one grave his wifes— the stone says in honor of

> (his wife's name I forget)
> a Cornish woman who
> loved these glens and their people

Walked on—(such a glorious gorgeous day as exhilarating as California) went to Catholic churchyard saw such a strange tombstone lying flat on ground with rude lettering in contrast to exquisitely carved words on others   It says

> + Charles Mc +
> Aluster's Bury-
> ing Place
> Here lies the body of (sic!) boddy
> John his son
> died 11th
> March 1803
> aged 18 years

> Your ship
> love is mor
> ed head and
> starn for a
> fuldiew

Curious devilish emblem *a goat*.

[RJ] ~~Mrs. McKillop's husband thought the boy had been a sailor, and the goat a mascot—sailors' pet—strange idea to~~

~~them, explained with much circumlocution—aboard the warship.~~

[UJ] What can the word FULDIEW[23] mean?

Saw a McAulay tombstone with their coat of arms on. Mostly obliterated but a foot or boot was at the top and at the bottom the motto *Dulce Periculum*.[24] In Iona they told us all Lords of the Isles have ships on tombstones. A McDonnell stone with very handsome coat of arms date 1816. Came home by long road past McFetridge shop. Missed footpath.

UJ Friday Aug 2. Another perfect day. Delightful drive along shore road via Larne to Belfast. Curious effect basalt and chalk mixture of rocks natural and used together in walls. Had work done on car. Bought books. War book for Donnan also Yeats & the long desired 2 vol of Bewick's British Birds with precious woodcuts. This was our 16th anniversary. Garth had heartache about a lot of books he saw at the bookstore that he coveted.

---

[23] A "fuldiew" is a sailor's wage.
[24] "Sweet Danger."

UJ Saturday. August 3. Rain part of day. High wind. Letter from
Biddy[25] & Miss White about houses. —Accepted Biddy's offer
of house from Sept 19–Oct 19 at £2/10 a week. Wrote 8 letters
& some cards. Went to Cushendall to buy supplies. When we
got home walked to churchyard to copy inscriptions. Went by
narrow raised footpath through fields. Went over river **brown**
deep brown. Cushendun means foot of brown river —went
through lovely blue flax field. —Have heard that the flax water
(water flax is soaked in) ought to be kept from streams—it
poisons the fish. Evening Mrs. McKillop brought milk. Talked
about that tombstone. She has never seen it although she has
been there all her life. Said her husband said the man had been
to sea in the Crimean War and the goat was a pet on the ship.
Not likely. She said, "O the grandson of that män McAlister
was a very talkative män—O he had a running tongue—Many
a time we had to be laughing at what he was at—*askirling* and
that." Said the people about here used to make processions
once in every few years to Shane O'Neils Cairn—she didn't
know whatever for. "Such a whim of people and sure what was
there to see. Just an old heap of stones." **[GJ]** also "Its that
family [Here Garth draws an arrow back up to "McAlister."]
was always talking great curiosities." The signposts here at the
road corners are called fingerposts.

DJ Sunday August 4 Very windy   Mother wrote 7 letters and a
postcard today. Garth wrote a letter to Aunt Edith and I wrote
one to Grandmother. Mother took a picture of Peter and Mike
in the morning and their father and mother in the afternoon.
Also pictures of the house. Took a walk up the lane beside our
house and then across the moor of heather and furze bushes.
When we got to the top of the hill we had a beautiful view of
Cushendun, up Glendun and Red Bay and Garron Point on

---

[25] Bridget "Biddy" O'Sullivan, niece of Ellen O'Sullivan and the owner of
"Kerry Vor," a house in Oxfordshire where the family stayed later in their
journey.

the other side. [UJ] {Magnificent black sky over black glens with brilliant sunshine nearby. Wind exhilarating. Sheep, geese, cows & horses on the high fields.}

DJ Monday, August 5 rained heavily in the night.
[UJ] Stayed at home until late PM planning trip. Walked a couple of miles just before dinner. [DJ] The pictures of the ass and the baby one came today. They came out nicely. Mother maled them to the woman at Achill right away.

DJ Tuesday, August 6 rainy here.
Started on our trip down south this morning. It rained steadily almost all day. Went through customs at Newry. Stopped at Monastirboice. Considered one of the most beiutiful church ruins in Ireland. There is a round tower and several Celtic crosses. One, one of the most perfect, and one, one of the largest. We spent the night at Drogheda. We saw Lawrence's Gate. It was very beutiful.

DJ Wednesday August 7
Went to Mellifont Abbey [UJ] a place as sweet and beautiful as its name standing alone beside a stream a mill at one time diverted the water through one of its towers. Beautiful carved doors & windows green close clipped grass between the broken walls all very quiet and far from the regular highways—yet an invisible care taken keeping each fragment carefully intact. Next to Newgrange past Nowth & Dowth both old mounds —an old woman has taken care of the place for 20 yrs. An enthusiast. Spends her days beside it in a little hut. Newgrange is a big mound with great trees on top of it. Were amazed to discover some of the enormous trees to be cherry trees. At the base of the mound is a fosse of small stones. A big cup & ring carved stone is by the entrance. Enormous standing stones encircled the mound about half still stand. Enter through narrow passage. Must stoop. Inside all of stone roof and all a round small chamber over 20 ft high—3 small

alcoves off it. In one a large sacrificial basin more than 3 ft in diameter, hollowed out & 2 small hollows for "knees of the victims" —Some carvings on the stones and a fern leaf beautifully carved. Old woman told of the distinguished people who came there & all they said— She said the gov't is about {begin next month} to excavate from another side & attempt to find other chambers as this chamber is only a small part of the mound. The year before the war she heard terrific crashes & fallings coming out of the mound one evening & experts think it must have been falling roof of another chamber. They hope to find treasure & remains of an ancient race. —This chamber had been plundered by Danes (history tells) then covered over—rediscovered by man taking stones from field for the road— I was unexpectedly very much impressed with this place. All through this country along the Boyne are *artificial* mounds— This is very beautiful rolling country—wooded & plenty of small streams. Past Slane Castle and many fine estates. —Saw Donoughmore Round Tower near Navan— unusual in having crucifixion carved over doorway. Past Bective Abbey, thru Kells with its fine Round Tower and old carved crosses a fine but broken one in Market Place. Saw St. Columbs house with its stone roof. One goes up a thin ladder to the vaulted ceiling *35 ft*—above tiny cells. He may have with his students written Book of Kells here— Outside of Kells about 1½ miles where we ate lunch is a thin high tower like a round tower with a sort of lantern top and observation platform—built by a Marquis of Headfort generations ago— no one knows why. Now to Trim a remarkable small town filled with castles and an abbey—as thrilling a place as we've seen— a queer dwarf had the key to castle & offered to let us in but we had to go on to Swords with its great round tower and beside it a square tower of nearly the same height built 150 yrs ago. Spent night at very fine big hotel. *Malahide* (such a word *Malahide!*) Lord Talbot de Malahide such a name! In evening rode out to grounds of Malahide Castle saw cricket game. Couldn't go *through* castle grounds—wrong day. After

Trim went to Hill of Tara—gazed on stone pillar & thought of ancient kings.

UJ Thurs, Aug 8. —Past St. Douloughs Church to Dublin. Stone roof. Saw well. Queer little misshapen fat cross by roadside. National Museum. Saw all kinds of interesting things. —Stone implements to furniture & jewels. Chief treasures *chalice*, *Cross of Cong*, Tara brooch, crozier. —Saw enormous golden torques found in Hill of Tara.

To Library of Trinity College to see Book of Kells—so beautiful & brilliant in coloring so unbelievably intricate in design. Saw a letter of Patrick Bronte with a few words in Charlottes writing pasted in & letters of Swift, Johnson, Goldsmith[26] etc. Saw a book with carved wooden cover oak wood from old ceiling of Library, book of letters from kings & queens & famous people to Miss (*Du Clear?*) who for years worked repairing most subtly the Book of Kells. On the cover is the coat of arms of her family & the raised coronet is set with the pearls & the gems of the rings Miss Du C wore while doing this work.

1 Clones—	14 Clondalkin—
2 Armoy—	15–16 Glendalough 2—
3 Drumcliffe—	17 Kilkenny—
4 Monasterboice—	18 Cashel—
5–6 Clonmacnoise 2—	19 Cloyne—
7 Swords—	20 Kilmacduagh
8 Kells—	(biggest stones)—
9 Donoughmore—	21 Ballydooley—
10 Turlough—	22 Waterloo?—
11 Devenish—	23 Nendrum—
12 Antrim—	24 Drumbo—[27]
13 Melick—	

---

[26] Jonathan Swift, Samuel Johnson, Oliver Goldsmith.
[27] These are the round towers that the family saw in Ireland. The following list records the towns on their third car trip through Ireland.

1006 miles

Knocknacarry, Ballymena, Antrim, Lurgan, Banbridge, Newry, Dundalk, Castlebellingham, Monasterboice^O, Drogheda^X, Mellifont Abbey, Battle of the Boyne Oldbridge, Slane, Newgrange, Navan, Donoughmore^O, Kells^O, Athboy, Trim, Bective Abbey, Hill of Tara, Dunshaughlin, Ratoath, Swords^O, Malahide^X, St. Doulough, Dublin, Clondalkin^O, Dublin, Rathmines, Blackrock, Bray, Roundwood, Laragh, Glendalough^{OOX}, Laragh, Rathdrum, Meeting of Waters, Avoca, Aughrim, Tinahely, Shillelagh, Tullow, Leighlinbridge, Kilkenny^O, Waterford^X, Clonmel, Cashel^O, Cahir, Fermoy, Midleton, Cloyne^O, Midleton, Cork, Blarney, Cork, Bandon^X, Bantry, Glengarriff, Kenmare, Muckross, Killarney^X, Abbeyfeale, Newcastle, Adare, Limerick, Ennis, Gort, Kilmacduagh^O, Ballylee, Coole Park, Kiltartan, Oranmore Castle, Galway^X, Cong, Moytura, The Neale! Ballinrobe, Moore Hall, Tuam, Roscommon, Longford, Castlepollard, Kells^{OX}, Ardee, Dundalk, Newry, Banbridge, Dromore, Hillsborough, Belfast, Carrickfergus, Larne, Glenarm, Cushendall, Knocknacarry.

We hate the great loaves of tasteless white bread here. How they eat it! We laughed— one big hotel we stopped (out of hours) for dinner and as we stood by the office window waitress came in & got keys from manageress & unlocked a *safe* and carefully took out— —*2* loaves of bread—this horrid great white bread!

To Phoenix Park—great empty place to Zoo. [**DJ**] Tall interesting secretary bird, met him walking about everywhere we went. The tigers lions and leopards very beiutiful and graceful, one jet black leopard. One lion had a very funny expression. Mother said it looked like a badly made toy. Two large elefants, several kangaroos one with a baby looking out of its pouch. There were a lot of monkies. One of them looked very human playing with a bottle top. There was a large aviary with alot of parrots, macaws and cocatoos in it. One kept saying "Polly water." We saw two large fruit bats hanging upside down by one leg. Many other animals, all very interesting. [UJ] To Clondalkin 4 miles away to see Round Tower. Then to Horse Show. [GJ] At the show we saw a lot of the nicest horses we had ever seen. At first we watched them trotting around the judging ring, but it was the first and probably the last chance that we would ever see any good jumping so went and watched them. Then look at horses in box stalls brood mares with colts and thorobreds. Enjoyed it very much. [UJ] Long beautiful ride through early evening to Glendalough—the most perfect place of our whole lovely trip. Came over mts into dark valley. Tall round tower dark against the darker hills—Black lakes between the mts—just beyond. Ruined churches & yews & old tombstones & an enormous plain old stone cross & St Kevins Kitchen small church with small round tower built in. Hotel very simple but *solid*. Perfect in service— Best trout ever tasted! from rushing mt. stream right through garden. —This place frequented by English nobility. Took walk after late dinner around tower & ruins. *Much more* beautiful than Killarney—

UJ Friday August 9. Went up the glen to lakes—then back & on our way. At turn of road as we studied our map car drove up and there were Mr. & Miss Palache[28] & Biddy O'S & — Richardson Berkeley professor. Long talk & met later at Meeting of Waters at Avoca. Planned further meeting at Killarney on Sunday. On road horrible Irishman nearly ran into us, then he got out of his car & assailed us loudly. He was surprised when we shouted back at him as red and fierce as himself. He had intended to impress us with his Irish temper. At Tullow was a crowded fair & a woman in street singing pathetic ballads in a quavering raucous voice. No one paid any attention to her. At Kilkenny a fine round tower rather lost being within a foot or so of a huge cathedral. An enormous

---

[28] Whitney Palache, vice president of the Hartford Insurance Company, and his daughter Helen, friends from Carmel.

castle. We could not enter as Earl of Ormond's family was in residence. Supper at Waterford. Long broad quay. Gazed upon Reginalds Tower on quay. Sent card to O'Shea. Night at Clonmel.

UJ Sat Aug 10 To Rock of Cashel— Magnificent ruins high on a hill with a fine round tower beside them. Saw famous cross, crucifixion on one side, St. Patrick on other—all on top of old Druid stone. —Cormac's tomb inside very fine carving. —We climbed to top of tower by long winding stair—magnificent view. —Saw finely carved door heads etc and bits of colored fresco in one chapel. Late in P.M. to Cloyne south of Cork. Saw round tower. —On to Blarney. We got off the road & drove & drove—finally found our way after much loss of time. Passed queer round tower at Waterloo (ancient?) of queer shape—curving in at top. Blarney so high and dim & gray and beautiful rising above the lovely green meadow. Ancient yew trees below. We climbed to top. —Boys thrilled. Pictures never reveal the high and dignified form of Blarney. Slept at Bandon—on over beautiful Glengarriff.

UJ Sunday August 11, Kenmare road to Killarney over mt. pass with wide fine views. Stopped at Muckross Abbey fine ruin with most ancient yew in cloisters. —Then we walked through grounds & hired a boatman for lake. He had been drinking & I did not feel very safe— the water was very rough from high wind and he later informed us the boat was designed to hold 2 (not 5!) Talked of owner Arthur Hill Vincent (estate at Pebble Beach). Wife died few months ago suddenly in New York. Showed us her fast rowboat in boat house. Saw her fine bulldog. Beautiful views all around lake. Rowed about for nearly 2 hrs. Night at Limerick. Asking a direction on our trip man said "O sure its only 2 wee short English miles." Saw a big field enclosed with wire threaded through hewn *stone* fence posts.

A place with a queer magical (black magical) name— Mooncoin.

Name of village amused us Kilmacow.

Often see carved stone pineapples on gate posts of manor houses.

Asking a direction to some town on a twisty road not well signed —again and again we were told "Go until you come to the fighting cock & ask there." —A public house it was with a vital & energetic cock painted on the sign board. Under it said "While I live I'll crow." [DJ] In its breast were [UJ] 3 bullet holes. —Everywhere we find these bullet holes got during the trouble. At the hotel in Glendalough 5 panes of glass in front door had bullet holes. Porter told beneath his breath of being besieged there & place shot up. [DJ] In another hotel there was a big bulet hole 3 in across a mirror.

UJ Monday Aug 12. To Gort & then several miles away to Kilmacduagh a very fine round tower & "seven churches" ruinous far away in a remote country region with fields divided by stone walls and bits of boggy water in little pools—and reeds growing among the stones—utterly lonely and desolate. {When we asked directions to this place of a peasant he said Go on —& "you'll see the spear!"} Cyclopean stone work & doorway here. This tower & the ones at Antrim & Glendalough are said to have been built by Gobán Saor. — Back to Gort—a crowded and lively cattle fair was in progress— boys got out & wandered amongst cows & sheep and little ass-carts and horses. On again to Ballylee, Yeats' tower & cottage. Lovely and quiet in the bright afternoon sunshine. All closely shut up pale green shutters, —in walled garden we could see little red apples ripening on the tree. Across the narrow lane from the tower & the five tiny cottages (in 2 tight rows) attached to it is another walled (low) garth with tall grass and young maple and beech trees planted and the rushing stream. A playground with cement floor & wall for dryness & a swing for his children also a small stone cottage

and garage together. Back to Gort then toward Galway. Drove
through grounds of Lady Gregory's *Coole Park*. Unpretentious
little white gate house, then a saw mill—they have been cutting
the great forest at Coole. —Up near the large rectangular white
house were enormous yew trees *covered* with beautiful red
berries. I hardly believed there were so many yew berries in the
world. —On through Kiltartan and fine dinner at Galway. —
Beautiful flat open country with groups of trees, ponds of still
water and many towers and ruined castles. Lovely late
afternoon sunshine & fleecy clouds. —To Cong where Cross
of Cong was wrought. Old market cross with Lombardic
characters— Beautiful abbey—such carvings! In adjoining
church pipe organ music swelling out. Boys playing handball
against wall by abbey. At other end of tiny street a mill with
great pond and fall of water through stone arches—the most
beautifully colored scene I've noted in Ireland. Sunset light,
clear pool, purple flowers along edge reflected in water white
geese and white clouds reflected, also white stones on the
grassy mound beyond. Sir Wm Wilde's estate Moytura is here
and beyond the old battlefield Moytura—passed a place called
the Neale. In churchyard a hideous high mountain of lava-like
porous rock with cavernous holes in it and over all great life
sized colored images of Christ, Mary Magdalen St. John etc in
various attitudes. —Mosaic like patterns on ground covered
with white ground stone big inscription about being erected by
the people of the Neale to show their love for their Saviour.
Slept at Ballinrobe. In evening a dirty fellow played most
sweetly & plaintively, wild sad airs on a little pipe. We threw
him a sixpence & he played on. We liked it very much &
thought of George Moore's shepherd & his playing The Wild
Goose in the mist. Forgot to mention as we stood gazing at the
images at the Neale there was a tremendous rushing like the
flowing of a great river over a fall—or a heavy wind through
the treetops—and looking up we saw thousands & thousands
of rooks blackening the sky—they had been frightened from

their rookery and sought another resting spot in the trees beyond us.

UJ Tuesday Aug 13. *Pouring* rain. At breakfast talked to Irish gentleman (gone a bit seedy)—perhaps the owner of the hotel. —He knew George & Maurice Moore. Talked about the ruined manor houses and the desolation through the country. Said he had never expected Moore Hall would be touched because of all Moore's father had done for Ireland— Said he thought it the spite of small farmers who wanted the estate divided into small rentable farms. To Moore Hall part of way on high narrow bog road—deluge of rain—took some good pictures and wandered through the house. Heard the same sad bird in the wood— Lake Carra very low and showing sandy bottom *many* wheel tracks at edge. Now all day we zig-zagged across the middle of Ireland through rain toward Roscommon. —Supper at Kells at Headfort Arms—very nice. Wished to stay the night but she had no place—full—on to wretched hotel at Dundalk. In Ardee we saw two small but perfectly proportioned castles in the main street. Saw here a fine half grown mastiff.

DJ Wednesday 14 August Crossed the border this morning early. Went to Belfast to give our R.A.C. papers back as we will not be going into the Free State again. All the way from Belfast it was bright sunshine and heavy rain alternately.

GJ Thursday 15 August **[UJ]** Today Teddie's[29] birthday. Also 10th anniversary of our moving into Tor House. **[GJ]** Showery during the morning but cleared up later in the day. Went to see the sports at Cushendun. When we got there a highland band was playing in the middle of the field. After it stopped came lot of foot races, men, and boys' and one girls' then a bicycle race, and they were just starting to play hurling when Father

---

[29] Edward "Teddie" Kuster, Una's first husband.

and Mother took us home. They had been hunting all over for us. After we went there was a horse race in which there were only two horses. One of the men was thrown but wasn't hurt. That and the boat racing were the only things we missed. [UJ] {Father found proofs of *Dear Judas* here when we came home & corrected them today.}

GJ Friday August 16th   Rainy all day. Read and drew. In the afternoon we went to Cushendall and I got a program for the coming cattle show. Mother bought a chicken but it was bad and we had to throw it away. It is interesting to see the people harvesting the flax (pulling the lint). After it is pulled the flax is piled in piles of about three sheaves where it is allowed to dry for about three days and then thrown in big ponds for ten days. Then it is sold. When Mother asked in the grocery for peas they said Oh yes, we will go out into the garden and *pull* them.

UJ Sat Aug 17. Got up at 6 drove through rosy early morning to Larne to meet Ellen O'Sullivan. She was to arrive at 8:25 was hour late owing to crowds for motor race at Belfast. Glad to see her. We went to Garron Tower for lunch— Fine old manor or small castle built by Marquis of Londonderry now a hotel. Has fine carved oak in halls. Beautiful gardens. Avenue of old yews. Some old cannons. —and an eucalyptus (first seen in Ireland) A fine view over sea from its high position & at its back black hills overhang. In P.M. to Ballycastle, Armoy & over Aura Mt. Some rain storms. Ellen thrilled with wild wide views. —Peat— Came back & walked with Ellen down to Cushendun where she is put up at Glendun Hotel. Very hard rain tonight. Hear our little brook go by with great purling down the glen.

UJ Sunday Aug 18. All went to lunch with Ellen at Glendun Hotel. Went first to old altar {the "Good Stone" brought from Iona or Staffa} in the woods near church, then after lunch we climbed to Shane O'Neil's Cairn then came back and watched the hurling game then drove to Parkmore by the great larch plantation beyond Cushendall and went into Glenariffe Glen and several miles deep in the glen along the course of the river, amber-brown with peat drippings, and beside fall after fall— one 100 ft high—Very fine & wild and gloomy. —Great ferns all along.

DJ Monday Aug 19 Went to Portrush with Ellen. Had lunch at a nice cafe. Then we went to Finvoy near Kilrea where there is a wonderful cromlech. It was about 6 feet high. Another was a huge flat stone about 18 in thick and 10 ft long by 8 ft. wide. It was supported by three upright stones. We think there used to be four legs one of which is lying beside it. About it are alot of standing stones and the remains of a stone circle. Mother found a bunch of white heather. [**GJ**] Ellen said it was in a more picturescue position than Stonehenge. It stood in the middle of a lonely heath and when we first came upon it we flushed about 25 grouse. I had never seen any before so after tea I went on top of a little rise to see if I could see any more, but didn't see any until I was coming back when one rose about 20 feet away and burred away across the heath. [**DJ**] At Portrush Mother bought a lovely bog-oak walking stick and a little compass made out of Connemara marble for us.
[**UJ**] Such a beautiful afternoon: the wide high rolling moor covered thickly with purple heather with a few pools of bog water—and here and there a thorn tree. —When the wind blows through one thorn tree—the sound is as the soughing of a whole forest— One old gray stone house stood alone at the edge of the moor—Robin thought it should be called Wuthering Heights— We walked for some distance—nearly a mile—then on a rise saw the cromlech—a most impressive massive one. —Above circled curlews calling plaintively and such beautiful windy clouds—pure white above but black and threatening in the west. —Far far away we saw the dim blue mountains—between us lay a smiling valley with little farms of grain & flax between. We had brought tea with us and after that I found a lucky bunch of white heather. —A group of

people came as we were leaving. The children were a pair of *twin* girls! On our way back as we left the rim we saw two peasants making a sod wall. They confirmed our belief that the *"Broadstone"* once had a fourth leg. A generation ago it had fallen & the top stone tilted & the estate owner McGinnis had with the help of the tenantry reset it firmly on 3 legs. Urns and other remains have been dug out there. Another small cromlech may be seen a half mile away. [**DJ**] The post mistress gave Mother a glass ball that they used during the war to hold up the sub. nets [**UJ**] nets to catch submarines. [**DJ**] We met at the Glendun hotel a relitive of Mr. Praeger. Her name was Armstrong.

DJ Tuesday Aug. 20— Mother wrote several letters. Garth wrote one postcard and I wrote 3 postcards. Had lunch at Glendun hotel with Ellen. Afterwards we fed the dux. There were over a dozen big ones, and about a dozen middle sized ones and four little ones that looked about one day old. Afterwards we went to Fair Head. We had to go over a lot of swampy ground, but it was worth it. Mother told Father and us to go to the next head and see if there was anything interesting. Every time after coming to one head there was another one more interesting. After awhile we found we had gone about a mile. We could see Rathlin Island stretched out like a map at our feet. On this Robert Bruce watched a spider spin a web across the entrance of his cave. At either end we could see a lighthouse, and father thought he could see the castle. We called Mother and Ellen to see. The latter got very dizzy and would not come near the cliff. We went on and found "grey mans path," a huge column of stone stretched across a very narrow gorge. A little way further we came to the best cliff yet. It was made of hard grey basalt that went sheer down 300 feet, from there it went down over 300 feet in a steeply sloping pile of huge boulders. Father held all of us while we lay down flat and looked over. On the highest head of all there was a huge stone weighing several tons. Father thought it must have been put there by man as there was no place for it to fall from. He called it the corner stone of Ireland— The north-eastern most corner. He chipped a little piece off. We could see Scotland stretching for hundreds of miles along the horizon. The ground was carpeted with heather and Mother found another spray of white heather. We saw two goats on the little artificial island. Father found a flint that he thought was worked. In the Dublin Museum almost all the stone axes etc. came from Co. Antrim. Asked Peter McKillop about the strange notches in the bridges. We have been wondering about them for a long time. He said people sharpened their knives on the bridges and wore them down.

DJ Wed. Aug 21. Misting. Ellen went away today to Belfast on the bus. **[GJ]** Mist developed into a steady rain. Went to the cattle show at about half past one. The pigs were all Ulster Whites, a very large breed with big ears and an extremely dished face. There were several litters of very small babies that looked about as big as rats. One of the sows that was separated from her litter grew very uneasy and started biting at the door of her pen. Her owner knew what she wanted and put her in with her babies they immediately flew at, and started suckling her, all except one who roamed around squealing pitifully because it could not find a teat to catch hold of. All the sheep were black-faced. The rams were very pretty with there beautiful spiral horns. There were about fifty cows and calves of various breeds and nine Galloway bulls of various ages. There were some very pretty colts and two year olds they were all very frisky but not vicious. The sheep dog trials were not very successful as none of the dogs that we saw were very well trained. One disadvantage that the dogs had was that their owners could not drive the sheep with them but had to stand at the pen gate calling and whistling instructions to their dogs.

One of the dogs was driving sheep when a strange dog shot out from the crowd and caught a sheep by the wool   the sheep gave a twist and flung the dog into the air and the sheep dog jumped onto and held him down until the owner came up and took the dog away. Each dog was allotted three sheep and was supposed to drive them between several pairs of posts and finally into a pen. When one dog was driving all its sheep broke and got away. Two of them were captured by the audience but one got away and ran down onto the rocks with a boy after it. It had been raining all the time and we were soaking wet. Before the sheep dog trials were over father came walking along and informed us that Mother had come with the car and two steamer-rugs and the port wine to warm us up. At home we had to soak our feet in warm water for a while.

DJ [Thursday] Aug 22. Yesterday Father went to the police station to register as we have been in Ireland for almost two months. [**UJ**] —Today we were told that Mr. Evans the Belfast policeman who sublets this cottage to us, would be down—so when I went to door & saw a tall stern policeman I welcomed him in as Mr. Evans. He walked in very dignified & portentous, acted very stern & reserved— Finally discovered it was Cushendall head of police come to interview us as aliens before granting our registration! Was glad to be an *innocent* alien! He went away apparently satisfied with our data. He thought it peculiar for husband & wife to have only one passport.

UJ Fri, Aug 23. Went to Belfast in pouring rain to get back £41.10/3 from R.A.C. which had been deposited to obtain our Free State triptique. Lots of red tape. Finally got it & shopped had car lubricated & in pouring rain started home via Island Magee. Lots of trouble finding "Druids Altar." It was in front of a big house completely covered with ivy & trailing geraniums. Looking at it from inside found it a very fine one but what a shame to make it look like a little summer house outside. [**RJ**] Then we looked for "The Rocking Stone" and after directions from half a dozen sympathetic people we saw it from afar and ploughed afoot through mud where a field broke down to the shore at Brown's Bay. It looked big enough and rockable enough. They say that even the approach of a criminal will set it vibrating, but the boys and I are too innocent, no quiver for all our united weights and efforts. So then to the "Gobbins" but they were so evidently less impressive than Fair Head that we didn't leave the car, and went home dissatisfied. [UJ] Still pouring rain.

RJ Sat., Aug 24. Beautiful walk to Torr Head, after driving a little beyond Cushendun. We never felt so much at home as here on the Cushleake coast, it is so much like our own "down the coast." Not so large nor so long, but the hills very similar, and very beautiful, in their plunge to flat sea. We saw a ring of dry stone wall, ten or twelve feet thick, like a cahir, around a single tree. A boy with a bicycle said there is a cave under it, but knew nothing more. It looks like a stone fort, but we must investigate a later day. —Culrani Church. Black bull. Pitiful snipe wounded by a hunter. The boys wanted me to catch and kill it, but I was too cowardly. [UJ] {Saw coastguard station on Torr Head from Fair Head & Murlough Bay (from south) as we saw it from north} {Should have mentioned watching the men drive a small flock of sheep along the narrow road ahead of us and the clever dog who knew so clearly all he should do and his happy face at his successful manoeuvers. It was very beautiful—the wild sea below with dark swirling clouds, —the heathery rocky moor, curlews crying above, and the sheep— what animal so ties together the country and human life— There were a few goats along the way too and always tall gallant gray and white geese dignified and clearly having a plan— (chickens are always at loose ends)}

RJ Sunday, Aug. 25. Walk from home by the Knocknacarry school house and the old road over the hill to Layde; and home the same way, because it was late, and Una tired from never going

to bed until 2 AM or almost. There was an old woman popped
out of a house just where Layde [UJ] lane goes down to the
graveyard and came up to us where we sat on the hedge. She
said with a quaint accent that she was looking for little sticks
to start her fire in the morning that times were changed—when
she was a girl they burned turf and the fire kept all night in the
ash and didn't need to be started with little sticks in the
morning but now she had to go out every night to find some
to start the sea coals in the morning— She said it's a fine day
just—and what is the date— Sure August is a grand month and
the harvest comes then and many a laugh she'd had because
she herself was born in August when everything was *plentiful*—
salmon in the bay and the harvest on the land. So she tottered
away down the narrow lane leaning on her stick and we heard
dry snapping of little twigs.

UJ Monday Aug 26   Word from Peter[30]   She would arrive
tomorrow morning in Larne. Went to Cushendall in P.M.
Mrs. McKaye kind soul gave us a fine chicken which we
cooked & enjoyed today. Boys went for cows tonight. Had a
hard time getting them they were put off the track by little
Hugh who claimed the cows went a different way than they
did. Came back with very red faces. They had had a hard time
"up the loaning."

DJ Tuesday Aug. 27   rain   Went early to Larne to get Peter. The
lovely chicken soup that we were going to have for lunch
turned souwer so went to Garron Tower. We noticed last time
we were there that the shades and curtons were painted onto
the glass. We found that the hotel was just a hollow shell like
Moore Hall and the windows were painted so we could not see
it. About a tenth of the place was inhabitable. After lunch we
went to Ballycastle and back by Armoy and Aura Mountain.

---

[30] Ella "Peter" Winter, writer and wife of Lincoln Steffens.

GJ Wednesday, August 28 rain Peter took several pictures. A sudden cloudburst almost drowned us but we managed to escape to a building. We saw the same beggar that we had seen the first time we went there. On the way back we had tea near Dunluce Castle. Then we went to Dunseverick, a little fishing hamlet which seemed very primitive. We saw the castle which just consisted of a ruined piece of wall. **[DJ]** Note Mother wants to put in how much she loves the bright blue eyes of the white geese. It is now the season for harvesting the flax "pulling the lint" as they call it. It is a very hard job. They have to pull it all by hand and tie it in bundles. They then take it to a small pond or "dub." It soaks there for ten days. The dub water is very poisonous and there is a £10 fine for draining it into the streem as it kills all the trout. However the farmers do it and we caught six sick trout yesterday (Aug 27). A few days ago all the men put on their old clothes, jumped into the pond and threw the bundles out. It has a terible smell like very strong old cheese. They do not use the seed for anything. After they take it out of the "dub" they untie the bundles and spread it out in the field to dry. After a few days they tie it up again and put in stacks, and let it dry some more. Then it is put on a truck and sent to the factory. Mother is the official photogrepher of the neighborhood. First Mother took a picture of the McKillops. Then she took a picture of Mac. K. Now Mr. John McDonald and a woman with 1 year old twins want Mother to take them.

GJ Thursday August 29 We had lunch with Peter at Cushendun. Before lunch we fed the ducklings and grown ducks about half a loaf of mouldy bread. Some geese also came to join in the repast. After lunch we took Peter to Larne to catch the train to Belfast on the way we had tea. All the way I was busy making a snare to catch a water rat.

DJ Friday Aug 30 rained all day. Mother washed her hair in the morning. I wrote a letter to Uncle Jerry and Aunt Daisy. In the afternoon we went to Cushendall and Father and we had our hair cut. We went back by Layde the way that we went along last Sunday to see if we could see Mercedes Gleitz swimming the chanal. We could not see her.

DJ Saturday Aug 31 some rain Father walked to Ossian's grave today. Had a long talk with John McDonald who told us about a lot of subteranian passages. We had our hair washed today. Mother wrote 16 letters and cards today. Learned that Mercedes Gleitz had to give up 3 miles outside Fair Head.

DJ Sunday Sep. 1 —shows signs of clearing up but still a lot of rain. There was a little bit of thunder and lightning last night. At lunch we found that a whole loaf of bread was moldy so we went down to Cushendun and fed the dux and duklings. Afterwards we went past Moira O'Neil's house to a little fishing cottage Mother wanted to take a picture of. There was a nice cottage that unlike most houses in Ireland had quite a few windows. Mother said that she would like to see the inside of it. While she was taking a picture of the fishing house a man came along and entered into conversation with us. He was an artist. When Mother came back he asked whether she would like to go into the house and see it. It was very nice inside and it had a bathroom. [**UJ**] {artist name Craig.[31] *Very* fine paintings gave us a start of surprise.} [**DJ**] Mother was too tired to go up to a ring fort that we saw on a hill beyond Shane O'Neil's cairn when we went to Torr Head. After going thru several fields we reached it. [**RJ**] Circular dry-stone walls, about nine or ten feet thick at the bottom and six at the top, battering chiefly on the outside. Seven or eight feet high in places, enclosing a green-sward sixty feet or so in diameter. On one side a half-blocked up little doorway, only three or four feet high, with a great one-stone lintel, gave entrance to a passage running both ways inside the wall. But we did not enter—no time for exploring.

---

[31] James Humbert Craig, Irish artist.

Inside the circle, against the wall opposite the entrance, a big maple or sycamore tree. Some deep straight furrows in the grassed earth, going straight across the circle, made us think that it had been trenched by excavators. The entrance was partially walled up, six feet or so wide, between the big stone jambs in the wall. If these jamb-stones were original (which I doubt) they didn't go up to an arch, for they battered away from each other. There are said to be caves underneath. Curious that we can find no notice of this structure, so near Cushendun.

DJ Monday Sept. 2. In the morning we went to the police station in Cushendall to see if our papers had come. They had not which is a great nuisance as we will have to give up our house tomorrow and we cannot leave here until we get them. In the afternoon we went to Ballycastle to see Bonamargy Abbey where most of the McDonald clan is buried, also the rock where the sons of Usna {& Deirdre}[32] landed. **[UJ]** Then we went along the road at foot of cliffs from Ballycastle to Fair Head. A lonely wild road with the sea almost washing over it. At the last wild bit, one small stone house most desolate & poor with an enclosed yard full of nettles. Inside we saw a woman & small child. A pair of gulls wings tacked on the wall. Outside at the edge of the water a boy fished for a tiny stick (for fuel.) We were here for 20 min & he had just got it as we left and ran happily to his mother with his salvage. —A worn and thin desperate man came staggering down the side of the hill with a bundle of wet reeds & began thatching the roof. — The feverish little light gleamed on and off from the small lighthouse **[DJ]** (In the evening Mrs. McKillop & Mike & Peter)[33] **[UJ]** at end of Rathlin Island. Fair Head was magnificent and dark—the hills dripped with water, the sea

---

[32] Added by Una.
[33] Written by Donnan before Una began her entry. She drew parentheses around Donnan's words.

was rising wild and dark—the dark caverns of those ancient
and abandoned coal mines showed their black throats.—
We drove hastily again to Cushendall police station. No sign of
our papers. Mrs. McKillop very funny. Told us tales of John
McDonald who goes crazy at this time each year & never is
without his fishing rod, meandering over the hills. Also startled
us by telling us at first in a very roundabout way about Alex
Martin's going crazy a week ago. {Said he was away in his
head} His brother has been sent for from America— We saw
him in a cart this morning sitting in bottom of it between 2
men & a brother driving. He looked queer and tragic. We all
spoke of it—how unnatural he looked. He is usually so gay and
full of talk. (Met an old man in road near Bonamargy who knew
all the country, asked us if we were antiquarians. Told us Sorley
Boy McDonald lies with 8 of his family in the deep vault in
Abbey iron doors put up by Lord Antrim. Told us of Deirdre
of the Gobán Saor's Castle and many other ancient things.
Robin spied an ancient stone cross leaning against the fence in
a grain field.
Drumnismere is name of townland next to Dromore ~~Peter
writes of an inn at Tewkesbury, called "Ye Ancient Grudge."~~
Near sighted woman at next table at Clarendon Hotel looked
out of window at sign across the street and said What an odd
combination piano tuner & funeral furnisher. —Sign is really
Adam Turner funeral furnisher.
Gortacraigin the McKillops house, Castlegreen (by McFetridge)
At Grey Abbey in the Ards—a beautiful old ruin near the town
of Grey Abbey—I copied several epitaphs one—
> "Here lyeth a patron of modesty, prudence and virtue, Martha
> Gibson wife etc."

One chapel was devoted to the Montgomery family a Lord
Montgomery 1677, —had a long epitaph. It had been carved
on a stone of Manx marble which was broken in 1843 by a
stone falling from the wall and replaced in the same year by a
member of that family with the epitaph recarved exactly— I

copy only fragments of it and even in these I was too hurried
to note all the queer spellings and capitals.

> Lord Montgomery & his wife
> — —Layd in ye vaulted tombe made for their peculiar
> Repository, his good & only wife and their only issue James
> . . . & (his children) God's lovely loans.
> Let then their bones and dust rest here untossed
> Others rooms having elsewhere nothings lost
> Intruders still graceless usurpers are
> Ones tombe belongs not even to his Heire.
> Them twice by God joined none but Hee may sever
> Th'are layd up Here 'til Hee raise them forever
> May all their Race be pious and safe keep
> This house & Bed where (in our Lord) they sleep
> Corpora dant Tumulo signant quoq Carmina
> Saxum qd impolitum donavit. Fra: Allen Arm."

Earlier in the epitaph it spoke of the above Saxum having come
from *Manx* Island.

> Epitaphum
> Sir James Montgomery by pirates shot and of them dead,
> 12th March 1651/2

[RJ]   And by the same solemnly burièd.
[UJ]   Apostrophe
> To the sub-aerial elements.
> Devouring Hades the ever-hungry earth
> Wouldst & shall eat up all thats of thy birth
> Faln in thy lap by death of any kind
> But whom the waters drink & last day find.
> Step to 1st Corinth. Ch XV, Verse 51
> Yet graves & waves must all such guests restore
> At that great day to live forevermore
> Tho he's deceased, his noble acts & name
> Longer than this can last shall live by fame.
> Prov. Chap. 22, V. 1. Eccl Ch VII verse 5
> So always pray and always pray ought we
> At my full height my length did not surpass

My father's shadow as at noon it was
Carmina mea tribuunt, fama perennis erit"

Another perished in the wreck of the SS Tweed on Alacranes
Reef in the Gulf of Mexico 1847 Another wounded in Battle
of Waterloo 1815
Another stone was to some servants of the family a ~~man~~
{woman} from Rome and ~~a~~ {her} Scotch ~~woman~~ {husband}.[34]

RJ Tues. Sept 3. Una finished packing, we all helped according to
our several powers; the trunks went off at 10 AM, but with
cleaning up etc., the family not before 3 PM. Torrents of rain.
At Cushendall the sergeant told me our papers had not come,
and "I'm not supposed to tell you, but since you are such a
gentleman!" he would send in a report to Lisburn and we could
get them there the next day. At Larne Una engaged passage for
the car and looked up the trunks. They had come unprotected
on top of the bus from Cushendall, and were apparently
soaked with rain. Una in despair. So instead of staying there
and going to England, the trunks must come to Belfast and be
dried at the hotel. They were promised to be delivered at the
Clarendon that evening; by means of two agitating visits to the
station we managed to get them by 8:30 next morning,
delivered on a laundry truck before the regular baggage truck
got under weigh.

RJ Wednesday, Sept 4. Una and I have awful headaches, from
going to bed very late, and (as to her) worrying sleepless about
the wet trunks; (as to me) getting up at seven and interviewing
station agents before my coffee. We are delicate blossoms.
Trunks opened and aired; no damage. We drove to Killinchy
cross-roads, then a mile to Killinchy village and the old wind-
mill, and a mile down to White Rock on the lough. There a
young man mending his boat told us it was three miles by the

---

[34] Robinson added the corrections.

lough shore to Nendrum Abbey on Island Mahee. Nendrum was a quite wonderful place, though there must have been little left of it before the restorers went to work. The cashel—encircling walls of dry-stone—reminded us of the fort at beyond Cushendun. On top of the hill, against the butt of the broken round-tower, a tremendous old horse stood dreaming. His head was weird and ancient to see; his right hind leg was swollen as big as a barrel, and the swelling went up under his belly. Una regarded him with horror, he looked at us thoughtfully and walked off a few paces. [**UJ**] {He was monstrous high & monstrous swollen, and of the strangest color dun—with large white spots—piebald.} [**RJ**] —On our way back the tide had come in and covered a raised road that led to the sixteenth century ruined castle at the other end of Mahee Island. We drove back through Killinchy to Florida Manor, and thence zig-zag to Lisburn where we visited the police station and got our papers at last. Then, asking directions right and left, to Drumbo, where the round tower is about as high as the one at Armoy, and stands, like that one, in a Church of Ireland churchyard. Then to Belfast. Our headaches were dreadful by this time.

UJ Thursday Sept. 5.[35] I gave up entirely and went to bed without my dinner. Robin went to dinner with boys who are the best travellers in the family. After hot water bottle at my feet & cold on head & aspirin I managed coffee & toast in bed, & woke up all right on *Thursday Sept 5*. Spent the morning in the Ards. Went to Grey Abbey—then drove on to Portaferry. Country most sweet & smiling and gentle, happy farmhouses and everything prosperous. Rich grain fields—grain being cut. Along the shore of Strangford Lough tide out—long bare stretch of mud. Turned at end of peninsula (Portaferry) came

---

[35] In the original diary, Una began her September 5th entry without a date. She added the date and underlined it where it is italicized five lines below.

back by Atlantic side. Bright sunshine. I love the sea. —We
had to hurry—even so didn't get back to lunch until 2:40. —
Rather a failure afterwards. Went to Lough Neagh outside
Antrim to cruise to Ram's Island—then to Antrim Round
Tower. [**RJ**] The boats go to R.'s Island only on Wednesdays,
and the tower can be visited only Wednesdays and Saturdays.
Returning, we saw by the way an extraordinary tumulus with a
rath about it, the rath was dug through and a passage led into
the mound. The place was fenced and private. Una stopped a
boy who was running a motor-roller on the new sidewalk.
"Would the people mind if we went in there?"— "Och, no."—
"It's open to the public?"— "No, but the owner is away, and
I just saw his wife go by on the bus. They'd never know if you
went in."— "Is there anything to see?"— "Ah, no.—
Darkness, just. It goes down ninety feet. They used to use it
for an ice house."— "Then there's nothing to see?"—
"Darkness just. But if you'd turn to the left and go up to So
and So's farmhouse—there's a tunnel through white rock that
comes out in the basement of a church half a mile away, and
they'd let you go in. It's grand scenery."— "What was the
tunnel made for?"— "Oh, for a hiding-hole or so. There was
a great battle here in Antrim and the ground is all full of holes
and hidings." But the rath having been used for an ice house
had chilled our interest, and we went to the Canadian-Pacific
office in Belfast, where Una learned that we must take passage
before Nov. 14 or after April, or else be landed at their winter
port, St. John's, with a long day's train journey from there to
Montreal or N.Y.

RJ Friday, September 6. In the morning we had the car lubricated,
and with Boots's help got the trunks shipped off to Larne. In
the afternoon we drove to the Giant's Ring, which is said to be

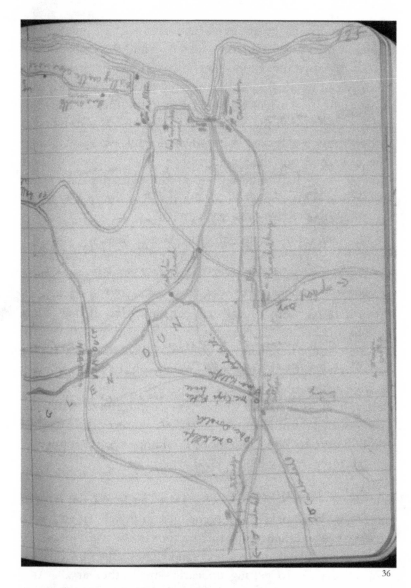

36

four miles from Belfast, but seems to be twenty, as it is on no regular road, and most of our informants knew the direction but dimly. It is a tremendous affair, a feeling of brutal ignorant

---

36 This map drawn by Robinson shows the area of the Glens of Antrim that the family used as their home-base while they were in Ireland.

power about it. A great circular embankment—I guessed the radius of the inner circle to be 80 yds.—and the embankment fifteen or more feet high—in the center a squat ponderous cromlech of basalt stones, the up tilted end of the slipped cap-stone eight or ten feet high. A great amphitheater with this heavy stone toad in the midst. The embankment is notched as if for entrance-gates—I counted six, I think I've read, seven. The boys had out their compass and found some of them oriented; we had entered ~~from~~ through the east gate. Inscription (Una copied it) on the five-foot stone wall about the outer edge of the embankment:

> "This wall, for the protection of the Giant's Ring, was erected MDCCCXLI by Arthur Third Viscount Dungannon, on whose estate this singular relique of antiquity is situated, and who earnestly recommends it to the care of his successors."

From here we went to Ballynahinch, intending if there were time to proceed to Maghera for a round tower or Ballynoe for a stone-circle. There was not time; we inquired the way to the Legananny cromlech, only 3 or 4 miles from Ballynahinch, but decided to give up that also; we had to get the car back to Belfast by 6:30 to have it washed. So we did, and walked back, losing our way a little among incredible slums of dirty women and children, to The Clarendon. To-night we must return for the car: tomorrow will be a day! Larne at 7:30.

RJ Saturday, September 7. We were to rise at a quarter of six, but did not wish to make the servants get up to call us; and as to breakfast, asked them to fill the thermos bottle with hot coffee in the evening and make a few sandwiches. But they insisted they were used to getting up early—no bother at all. At a quarter of six precisely Una's mental alarm-clock waked her, and after she had waked me, I heard the chamber-maid's alarm-clock ringing up-stairs—less effectively, for the girl never appeared. I went down and searched among the keys and found the garage key for myself. The "garage" is an old archway, in which a kitten lives, who spends her night walking all over the car with muddy little pads. When I had brought out the car and begun packing it, "Boots" appeared. He does not sleep at the hotel, so he alone escaped the debility of those Ultonians, and saw us depart. They had made no coffee, either. At Larne we got some, at The Towers hotel, run by the sister of Miss Burke of The Clarendon. Miss Burke of The Towers, after she heard our story, would take no payment for the coffee. —We reached Larne half an hour ahead of time, and saw the car hoisted aboard. Hours later, ourselves got aboard and were rather soon at Stranraer. But it was past noon before the trunks were sent off to England, by goods train, and the car hoisted out. We went northward, through a happier looking country than Ireland, and landscapes and shores as beautiful. Ballantrae, where we met a baker's van, scones of ginger-bread for lunch; Ayr—streets like the streets in an ant-hill, and Una insisted on driving about to Alloway and taking the boys into Burns' birth-cottage. Irvine—a good meat-tea in a second-class hotel. Lugton—Caldwell—a little tower on a hill, which turned out to be Chryssie[37] Allan's tower—Uplawmoor—a cottage and a great beech-tree. Chryssie is extraordinarily generous and hospitable; her dog barks enormously without ceasing. About nine o'clock we had to eat another supper. The boys were put to bed in their shake-down.

RJ Sunday, Sept. 8. I think Chryssie would have liked us to go to church, but she says that she doesn't go often. We got up late, and spent much of the morning in her really wonderful old tower of Caldwell. Two barrel-vaulted ceilings and an embattled roof. In the three-foot walls, door after door and window after window built in and cut through by generation after generation of remodellers. The tower is five or six hundred years old, she believes and it looks it, and has had

---

[37] Christina "Chrissie" Allan, sister of John Allan, the husband of Una's half-sister Edith.

some history. It is one of her great enthusiasms. She'd like to live in it; and we quite understand. —In the afternoon we drove with her to Portencross by the sea—splendid sandstone sea-rocks—time-grown cobble on them—mountains of Arran island and the others offshore. [**UJ**] {Twirling chimney pots called "Grannies." Cranes in fireplace called *swees*}

UJ Monday Sept 9. Forgot to say we saw the head of Queen Elizabeth on cave hill in Belfast—the outline extraordinary likeness. —Donnan said in great disgust today *"Hootie!* When I point out a cripple now Garth won't even look!" —When we first came over the boys were *amazed* at the no. of cripples. Got away from Chrissies late with a good lunch along with us. At first lots of small towns busy & new-looking & uninteresting— then a drive of many many miles along the beautiful wooded shores of Loch Lomond over *Rest* & *be Thankful* Mt (after going through grim & gloomy Pass of Brander)—a magnificent scene. —then came a mt. with a stone monument on top with the most sweeping outlook—a circular roofless tower with megalithic pillars & lintels of granite dedicated in English & Gaelic to Duncan McIntyre the Glenorchy poet died in 1812. In ground in front was a rude *old* stone cross cut in a stone lying flat half-buried. —Before this pass we had gone to Inverary the Duke of Argylls place on Loch Fyne. Very wooded & beautiful deer forest. Now we are seeing shaggy long-horned Highland cattle. On through a long sunset to Oban, with its crescent beach & gay esplanade. Many men in kilts; the Highland Games start Sept 12.

UJ Tues. Sept 10 [**DJ**] Started at eight a.m. for the isles of Staffa and Iona on the little paddlewheel steamer [**UJ**] Freselier. [**DJ**] We stopped for a minute at Tobermory where a Spanish galleon {the *Florida*}[38] was sunk and there still is a lot of treasure in the harbor. We reached Staffa at about noon. It was

---

[38] Added by Una.

just like the Giants Causeway only the sections are a little bit bigger. We went into Fingals Cave along the side, it was too wavy to go in on the boat. The cave was about 150 feet long. The ceiling was supported on both sides by columns like the organ pipes at the Giants Causeway. [UJ] After an hours stay we went on to Iona by boat again. Saw the nunnery, cathedral & the old tombs. The tombs of the kings 28 Scottish, {many Irish,} several ~~Eng.~~ {Norwegian} & an unnamed ~~Scotch~~ {French}[39] king. Many traditions and relics of St. Columba here. His pillow (a stone) his head rested on after death—
A man & woman here do exquisite work in silver—crosses, & brooches—all copies of designs here on the tombstones {I bought 4 crosses}—a few very beautiful old crosses here—the McLean one. There is a plot of buried McLeans in a row 3 of them stone images of McLeans— Onto the boat again at 3 and back at Oban by 6 a beautiful day—the *Hebrides* have always been an enchanted place to me—and I did not tire of gazing at their wild rocky shores and misty hills. Going out & coming back looked at Dunollie Castle a mile from Oban along the road by the sea. Many castle ruins on the various islands today. —McCaig's Folly a colosseum rises high above the town. Ellen told us of a church in the Highlands where the shepherds went and stacked up their crooks—a great pile by the door. In Iona cemetery the old stones carved with ships indicate tombs of the Lords of the Isles or their descendants.

DJ Wed. Sept. 11 Started for John O'Groats today. We had to go over a high railway bridge over a lough at Connel ferry. We waited and waited and pushed the bell over and over the man would not come to open the gate. A Q of six cars formed before he came. 30 cars had come on the other side. We had to pay 10/6d. for going over the bridge. We paid 6d. for going over a ferry at Renfrew near Glasgow. We saw a very tall pillar stone in a grain field. We passed a big ruined castle called

---

[39] The corrections to Una's entry were made by Robinson.

Urquhart. We crossed a ferry at Ballachulish. Mother had to
drive her car onto a sort of turn table on a small boat. It looked
very dangerous. By the roadside there was a monument with
seven heads held by their hair by a hand with a knife thrugh
the hair. It was written in Gaelic, French, Latin and English.
Beneath it was a spring.

[RJ]   As a memorial
                          of the ample and summary
                                Vengeance
                       which in the swift course of
                             Feudal Justice
                        inflicted by the orders of
                     the Lord McDonnell and Aruss
                      overtook the perpetrators of
                            the foul murder
                       of the Keppoch family
                  a branch of the powerful and illustrious
                                  Clan
                        of which his lordship was
                              the Chief
                     this monument is erected by
                  Colonel McDonnell of Glengarry
                       XVII Mac-Mhic-Alaister
                     his successor and representative
                        in the year of our Lord
                                  1812.
                    The heads of the seven murderers
                     were presented at the feet of
                            the noble chief
                        in Glengarry Castle
               after having been washed in this spring
                       and ever since that event
                        which took place early in
                         the sixteenth century
                         it has been known by
                            the name of
                    Tobar-nan-Cleann—or
                      the Well of the Heads.

{The Latin version more detailed, flowery and rhetorical.}
[DJ] We had dinner at Inverness where there is a nice big castle. Then we went on to Dingwall to stay for the night where an old weasond and hunchbacked chamber made with St. Vitus Dance made up our beds. The moon looked very queer tonight. It was exactly a half moon ◗. We looked away for a minute and when we looked back it was a quarter moon ◺. A very dark and dense cloud had obscured the upper half. Afterwards it changed shapes like ◖ and △. The stars look very queer over here. [UJ] The constellations seem in the wrong place.

[RJ]   To mark the spot near which
                       about the year 1700
              the last wolf in Sutherland was killed
                   By the hunter Polson
               erected by the Duke of Sutherland—etc.
                          {near Brora}[40]

Staghorns [ ] Birches and evergreens deer lighthouse
[UJ] The fingerposts said "To Inverness & the North"— After Inverness *"To the North."* [RJ] Mud-guards and hub-cap crumpled opposite a pillar-stone by a cemetery, 2 1/5 miles beyond Bonar Bridge, going north. Thursday, Sept. 12.
[UJ] Culloden Moor battle of Culloden Apr 1746. Old granite unshaped slabs with names of different clans— Old stone spring with stone marked "Well of the Dead Here the chief of the McGillivray fell"— Farther along in a field apart separated by stone wall stone says "Field of the English—here they are buried"— Gray desolate country & dead heather—a bitter wind blowing— [RJ] Mounds of the dead. And great high cairn.

DJ Thur Sept 12 We saw 4 piller stones today, one very tall, about 12 feet. One of them Mother was looking at so hard she ran into a ditch and against a stone wall knocking the front wheel

---

[40] Added by Una.

hub cap off and bending both mud guards. Saw a stone marking the place where the last wolf was killed. A huge stag was standing beside the road. We stopped and watched it. In a little while two does and a fawn joined it and they all trotted over the crest of the hill. On top of a hill, silloetted against the sky several strange arches.

We could not immagin what they were. We stopped and asked a man. He acted very stupid but at last said there was an old monument up there. In an old cemetery [**UJ**] {near Tain} [**DJ**] by a church we saw a tower slightly like the Irish round towers. It said on it "Beigit 1616." Mother took a picture of it. We had supper at John O'Groats. We went back to Helmsdale to stay for the night. On the way about a dozen albitross ran across the road. [**UJ**] We saw a number of houses with deer horns dozens of them set along in rows. The houses & country have a Scandinavian expression. All houses of stone some ornamental wood work, pillars logs of trees with knots, (oiled) all very clean. Wild about John O'Groats few trees ~~Shetland~~ Orkney Islands close by—North Sea tossing between, 3 lighthouses gleamed in the evening along the coast. High hills covered with heather. Some rain. Gazed about for remains of Pict village. Thought we saw it. Went on & on until we came back to Helmsdale for the night. Frost in the night. Air very fine. Forgot my hot water bottle in the bed here.

UJ Friday Sept 13 Hubcap mended at Inverness. We had another fine hot supper at Royal Hotel & spent an hour in the antique shop. Saw a seal with 3 unicorns on it I wanted, too expensive, also looked at 2 skene dhu with cairngorm set in for boys. Ordered Lindsay plaid scarf & made arrangements to get Lindsay shawls if I want. Went on to Culloden Moor 2 miles off road, all wild & desolate, went on into Cairngorm mts,

beautiful wild & wooded. Went into dark spruce forest &
walked around on deep soft brilliant green moss beneath **dark**
trees, black trunks. Moon came up. At Oban forgot to mention
the Highland Games were in progress and dozens of fine
Scotchmen in full Highland dress were always in sight. Very
fine men too & a fine sight to see in their tartans. I love the icy
blue eyes & cold proud faces of the Scotch aristocrats—& his
fine haughty gait.

DJ Sat. Sept 14. Just after we left Pitlochry we were crossing a wide
moor when we saw a row of men about 15 feet apart going
across it, waving red and white flags to scare up grouse. Behind
were ate "noble" huntsmen in little black blinds. Probly they
pade thousands of £ to prictice this babyish sport. Just hide in
their blinds waiting for the line of shouting men to scare up the
grouse, and then bang! and down comes a bird. Father said he
would just as soon go out and shoot chickens. **[RJ]** {Ponies
with wicker panniers to carry the game.}

Belfast[41]	Kilbride	By Steamer
Larne	Portencross	Oban
Stranraer	Barrhead	Sound of Mull
Ballantrae	Paisley	Tobermory
Girvan	Renfrew	Staffa
Maybole	(Ferry)	Iona
Ayr	Dumbarton by	Firth of Lorn
Irvine	Loch Lomond	Oban
Dalry	Arrochar	
Beith	Inveraray	Railway Bridge
Lugton	Dalmally	Connel Ferry
Caldwell	Taynuilt	(10/6!)
Uplawmoor	Oban	Ballachulish

[41] This listing of towns was divided into two lists in the diary, the second
list beginning with "Elland." Una added a marginal note on p. 143 of the
diary where the first list ends, reading, "con. on page 184."

Ferry
Fort William
Fort Augustus
Drumnadrochit
Inverness^X
Beauly
Dingwall
Evanton
Alness
Kildary
Tain
Kincardine
Bonar Bridge
Clashmore
Golspie
Brora
Helmsdale
Lybster
Wick
John O'Groats^X
Wick
Lybster
Helmsdale
Brora
Golspie
Bonar Bridge
Kincardine
Stittenham
Evanton
Dingwall
Beauly
Inverness^X
  (Hubcap
  mended)
Culloden Moor
Moy
Carrbridge
Aviemore

Kingussie
Newtonmore
Dalwhinnie
Blair Atholl
Killiecrankie
Pitlochry
Kirkmichael
Bridge of Cally
Blairgowrie
Kirriemuir
Tannadice
Brechin
Forfar
Glamis
Meigle
Cowper Angus
Perth
Crieff^X
Comrie
St. Fillan's
Lochearnhead
Strathyre
Pass of Leny
Callander
Trossachs
Brig o' Turk
back to Callander
Aberfoyle
Rob Roy's Inn
Inversnaid
back to
  Aberfoyle
Strathblane
Milngavie
Maryhill Road
Renfield Street
Jamaica Bridge
Pollackshaw's

Road
Barrhead,
Uplawmoor
Barrhead
Paisley
Renfrew Ferry
Dumbarton
Helensburgh
Garelochhead
Arrochar
Rest-and-be-
  Thankful Hill
Cairndow
Inveraray
Lochgair
Lochgilphead
Ardrishaig
Tarbert
Ardrishaig
Inveraray
Arrochar
Loch Lomond
Balloch
Dumbarton
Renfrew Ferry
Paisley
Barrhead
Uplawmoor
Uplawmoor
Barrhead
East Kilbride
Hamilton
Motherwell
Coatbridge
Blackburn
Bathgate
Broxburn
Corstorphine

<u>Edinburgh</u>	Keswick	Twycross
Dalkieth	Thirlmere	Atherstone
Stow	Grasmere	Nuneaton
Galashiels	Ambleside	Coventry
Abbotsford	Windermere	Kenilworth
Melrose	Kendal	Warwick
Dryburgh	Old Hutton	Stratford on
<u>Melrose</u>	Kirkby Lonsdale	Avon
Abbotsford	Settle	Moreton-in-the-
Melrose	Skipton	Marsh
St Boswells	Keighley	<u>Stow on the</u>
Jedburgh	Haworth	<u>Wold</u>^{X}
Carter Bar	Lees	Crossed Hands
Byrness	<u>Halifax</u>^{X}	Pub
Rochester	Elland	Rollright Stones
Otterburn	Huddersfield	Enstone
Bellingham	Holmfirth	Woodstock
Chollerford	Penistone	Oxford
Roman Wall	Sheffield	Watlington
Greenhead	Chesterfield	Britwell Salome
Brampton	Clay Cross	Watlington
Plumpton Head	Alfreton	"Lambert Arms"
Penrith^X	Ripley	High Wycombe
Penruddock	Derby	Beaconsfield
<u>Keswick</u>	Ashby de la	Uxbridge
Druid's Ring	Zouch	<u>London</u>

[GJ] On the way to Inversnaid we saw three pheasants sneaking along by the fence. And farther on we saw about 10 grouse standing in a patch bare of heather. When we were going back I saw another pheasant. The day before, we saw a pheasant fly over a fence. [RJ] The Highlands are full of visitors, and on Friday (Sept. 13) we had rather a chase to find shelter for the night. At Dalwhinnie the big hotel, to which we were guided by signs, had burned down; we were directed to another and it had no room left. In the next village the hotel was full, the manager accompanied us to the station-master's house, but there the spare room had only one bed. She referred us to a hotel a few miles farther south, which we missed in the dark. At Blair Atholl all the hotels were full; at Pitlochry the first hotel was full, at the second we got a room.

RJ Saturday, September 14. Through mountains along the Ardle Water from Pitlochry to Blairgowrie; through the weavers' town Kirriemuir to Brechin, where we routed out the beadle of King David's Cathedral and persuaded him to show us the round tower. More ornate roof than the Irish ones; and a doorway carved in relief with a peculiar crucifixion above, a saint on each jamb, and a beast from the apocalypse at the foot of each jamb. 106 feet and 7 inches high. Appearance quite unlike any Irish one, on account of the four-gabled stone roof, which projects a little at the eaves, and was not a round cone but octagonal I think. It was very like, in effect though not in size, to the little one attached to the church near Tain, "Beigit 1616," and like that one full of pigeons. This tall one is dwarfed by the juxtaposed equally high cathedral spire; and the "restorers" of a century ago widened the cathedral to include part of the round-tower base. It is built of big somewhat polygonal blocks of red sandstone. Three round towers in Scotland; Brechin, Abernethy, (near Perth), and a stump in the Shetland Isles. **[UJ]** Near Perth went through most perfect & beautiful old manor house called Huntingtower. {Paper flowered with plums & *sprays*. Little fireplace with quaint bits of china above & 4 priceless rosewood chairs} Further on a house of stone exactly the shape of Tor House except for dormers (which we have planned also) Very *dear*. **[RJ]** From Brechin westward again; Forfar; Glamis, where we admired the estate entrance with its armless wild men and tiny hidden gate-house, all neglected and ancient; and gazed over the wall at the distant towers; Perth, where we bought coffee and wine, and saw with the pleased boys the North Inch and Fair Maid's House. At Lochearnhead we begged at half a dozen hotels and boarding-houses but could find no room; on to Strathyre in the dark, where we found the prettiest room yet, and good attendance, in a Temperance hotel. The place was well filled, but ours was the only car in the garage. [UJ] {At Brechin saw the oldest house there gray stone belonged to David Lindsay keeper of the keys.}

RJ Sunday, September 15. By Callander into the Trossachs, very pretty and soft and tame; back by Callander (no other road) to Aberfoyle, where the boys enjoyed Bailie Nicol Jarvie's hotel and Jean McAlpin's inn; then pitched up hill and down by pretty lakes to Inversnaid and back. The trees are soft, the waters and the skies and even the rocks a bit soft; the only grand scenery in these islands in the high waste moors, the far north, and the bare sea-islands. The rest is a feather-bed. Going home from Aberfoyle we lost ourselves in ugly Glasgow, asked our way of a policeman and others, and had to change a tire in the most crowded street. We've picked up more tacks and nails in a week of Scotland than all our months in Ireland.

RJ Monday, September 16, Una washed clothes, and rested a little in the afternoon.

RJ Tuesday, September 17. Long drive to Tarbert and back, 10 AM to 10 PM. Bad roads and much tire-trouble. Rest-and-be-Thankful Hill in Inveraray again. Tarbert a lovely little place, with its loch-harbor, from whence we brought back stones for Chryssie and Allan. Went by Helensburgh, (Clyde Firth and Gare Loch), back by Loch Lomond, made interesting by the great low scarlet harvest moon on its far hills. From Balloch to Uplawmoor, almost continuous factory town; incredible never-ending slow streams of sauntering young men and women in the early night.

RJ Wednesday, September 18. Chrissie off to Spain early this morning, leaving us in possession of her house. She is very kind. We start to-morrow morning; to-day, preparation etc. I took some tires to the foot of the hill to be fixed, and coming

back passed a four or five-year-old child staggering ~~and panting~~
up the path. I said "Hello." She: "I have to gae sae fast!" I said
"It's pretty wet, isn't it?" She, panting: "I have to gae sae fast!
because I have to gae to Mrs. Bro<u>cht</u>y's" (tremendous guttural)
"before I gae tae skule." Drizzling misty rain most of the day.
[UJ] While we ate our lunch near Aberfoyle Robin found a
long narrow stone like a pillar stone & after eating worked hard
with boys help & set it on end in the ground & made a bracing
foundation of small stones—& so made another monument in
these mountains!
How clean and self respecting all the Scotch villages—and how
excellent the food—such cakes & bread. —
Robin washed car— Later sun came out. Went up to little
Uplawmoor Inn to put car in garage—the darlingest inn
straight out of a story book—*clean*, white washed stone with
bright green paint around windows & doors—bright curtains,
& inside a stone floor, old polished (with use) benches & table
pewter & brass & shining glass & old china. A rosy plump
smiling woman serving ale to two men who sat at a ~~big~~ long
oak table, a great fire of sea coals & enormous crane (suie)
hanging over fire. Walked back, Peter got into a fight— Robin
pulled dogs apart, clear frosty air very invigorating. Uplawmoor
a charming village old houses & some new stone, full of
windows and comfort & snug self-contained family life. —
Supper, reading, baths & to bed.

UJ Thurs. Sept 19. ***Rain***—to Edinburgh after cleaning house.
    Peter sad and pining. Left him chained up until Chrissie's sister
    should arrive.
    {Mary Queen of Scots bedroom—where she gave birth to
    James VI, tiny paneled room *black* oak. Unicorns painted on
    the wall & between them this prayer of hers printed}
    —in the Castle

         Lord Jesu Chryst that crount was with Thornse
         Preserve the Birth, quhars Badgie heir is borne
         And send Hir sone successione to Reigne still

Lang in this Realme, if that it be thy will
Als grant, O Lord, quhatever of Hir proseed
Be to thy Glorie, Honer and Pease. Sobied.
19 Iunii, 1566[42]

Went along Princes St to ~~castle~~ Holyroodhouse— Saw Queen Mary's rooms etc place where Rizzio was slain, little supper room, Mortlake tapestries then Queen's Drive all around the treeless King's Park—wild spot to be *in* city. 2 small lakes. ~~King~~ Arthur's Seat fine view of city—back through Canongate past Tolbooth, & to John Knox's house, then to zoo for a quick [**RJ**] recognizance by Garth and Donnan. Rather meagre dinner. Then we unpack the car, partially, and take it to garage for the night, and to have a hesitancy corrected that it has suffered from for two days. The garage recommended by the hotel was a couple of miles away—"Oh, only five minutes," they said, and added " . . . by car"—we demanded a nearer one—got almost irretrievably lost in finding it, and walking back to the hotel saw a man throw his hands to his head and collapse in the street. Incredible pallor of his face. He arranged his limbs as if for burial, after he had fallen. Men picked him up, a crowd gathered and increased, Garth and Donnan were fascinated. After ten minutes two policemen came and began stirring the crowd back and forth like spoons in porridge. At length the ambulance: and so to bed. [**UJ**] When we drove into the courtyard of Holyrood House boys exclaimed with glee— "O—see the stuffed Highlander!" Sure enough in a tiny sentry box across the enormous courtyard was an apparently fatly stuffed Highlander (perfectly motionless sentry).

UJ Friday Sept 20 Shopped in vain for plaids & seals. Met Helen Freeland's husband on Princes Street. Bought a skene dhu with a Cairngorm in handle for boys & me. Went over the Castle.

---

[42] Una did not copy this prayer exactly. There are minor spelling and punctuation errors and one notable word error: she wrote "Pease" in the final line of the prayer; the correct word is "Prais."

Wild cold wind but sunny. [RJ] Gazed from the window
whence "James the sixth of Scotland and the first of England
was lowered in a basket" etc. Retrieved the car and went to the
museum of antiquities, where Una {(and we)} was especially
interested in —embroidered hawk's hood and glove for
hawking —tiny coffins with human-appearing corpses in
them— dolls four or five inches long. Eight of a horde of
seventeen found in a cranny of Arthur's Seat —carved ivory
table-man from DONNAN Castle, Ross-shire —key found by
Walter Scott in Loch Leven —Queen Mary's harp —gold
Unicorn and half-unicorn —ancient carved ivory chessmen
from Uist in the Hebrides, found in a subterranean chamber
uncovered by the sea —luck charms and charms against
witchcraft etc. (shrunken calf's heart stuck full of pins —holed
pebbles —mare's stone hung from bedpost to prevent
nightmare)—s— several amber beads worn by the Lady of
Glencoe on the morning of the massacre —G. and D.
interested in the spurs for fighting-cocks —round pattern-
carved stone balls so many of which were found in one
neighborhood in Scotland—and nowhere else—purpose
unknown— —bronze amulets of a type found only within 20
miles of the coast near Wick and Thurso—nowhere else. [UJ]
Went on then to Melrose for night at Abbey Hotel. At
Dryburgh Abbey a few miles from Melrose just before sunset
saw Earl Haig's headstone very simple upright slab with cross
on it (outside the rail a brass tablet mentioned that it was ~~like~~
identical with many others of his comrades in arms who died
in other countries). On footstone some device (baronial I think
& "Betyde what may") A small marble cross prone in grass of
a child member of Haig family of long ago. This is the Haig
burial plot next to Walter Scotts & his wife & son and Lockhart
Scotts son-in-law friend & biographer who "lies at the feet of
Scott." Beautiful cedars of Lebanon mixed with English &
Irish yews all across this beautiful ~~place~~ park.
Found my signature of June 1912 in the big register at Abbey
Hotel. Gave all of us a queer feeling. Boys overcome with joy

at the Museum of Natural History at hotel, hundreds of stuffed birds. An American woman who looked like Ann Dare here with English girl who is acting as her chauffeur & guide. She said just now to English girl "And what are you going to take me to in the morning—Shakespeare's birthplace?" No wonder we are caricatured *maliciously* sometimes over here.

[RJ] TRIMONTIUM/Here once stood the/Fort of Trimontium/ built by the troops/of Agricola in the/first century A. D./ abandoned at least / twice by the Romans / and ultimately lost by them after fully one hundred years/of frontier warfare.

[UJ] On a pillar set by roadside not far from Dryburgh

UJ Sat Sept 21. After breakfast went into Abbey grounds right adjoining hotel. On tombstones at Melrose

---

Be ye also ready, the small and great are here (on stone of tenant farmer in Drygrange Mill died 1791 age 70)

Here lyes all thats subject to mortality . . .

Robert Boston sometime farmer at Langshaw Etc.
The Dust of many generations of Bostons of Gattonside is deposited in this place. We give our bodies to the Holy Abbey to keep

---

Esq. of Sorrowless Fields—

Heir lyis the race of ye Hous of Zair

(& beneath emblems a candlesnuffer over a skull/stag head)

Such exquisite tracery & carvings here and the building of pale rose sandstone. Next drove to Abbotsford. Saw the rooms of Sir Walter & all the relics Rob Roy etc —also the inlaid with mother-of-pearl cross Queen Mary used on way to scaffold, skene dhu of Rob Roy, bog oak snuff box Maria Edgeworth gave Sir Walter. Wonderful guns & weapons, spirited wild looking portrait of his soldier son (showing his French blood plainly). We found everything extremely interesting after our last winter's reading of the Waverly novels & Lockhart's life of S. Around hall are painted rows of coats of arms & there is carved this line

> "These be the coat armouris of ye clannis and men of name quha keepit the Scottish Marches in ye days of auld."

[**DJ**] In the hotel [The Abbey Hotel] was a museum. In it were stuffed foxes, monkeys, a crockadile, duck billed platapus, otter, ermine, hare, pheasants, pea fowl, swan, heron, and several hundred more animals. Also all kinds of weapons. There were interesting stones and stones from famous places. There were coins and paper money from almost every country. There was a mumified hand and a hawk from an Egyptian tomb. What interested me most was an egg grenade, a mills bomb and another kind of hand grenade and three artillery shells one of which was the famous French 15 mm, two caps off "heavies" and French, Turkish, British and German rifle ammunition.

[**UJ**] Looked at trees Sir Walter planted. Through Jedburgh— (famous for keeping peace on the border). Queen Marys house there. Fine abbey. {Houses so beautiful throughout the country pale rose sandstone—even sometimes the roof of slates of same.} [**DJ**] The Cheviots were very wild and barren. The wind was blowing so hard it seemed as though it would blow the car off the road. On the road from Chollerford to Carlisle, the Roman wall was beside the road for several miles. [**UJ**] {Saw street called Bold Venture Street. Beside in the library at Abbotsford stood a man who was pointing out the portrait of Claverhouse—said "an ancestor of mine."} [**DJ**] We stopped at Keswick for the night.

DJ Sunday Sept 22. rained in the morning. Went to a place called the Druids Ring about a mile from Keswick. There are forty odd stones in it. [**GJ**] We saw a lot of young pheasants the other day in a field. About 30. [**DJ**] Near Inverness there are about nine German guns, most of them are about 75 mm. [**UJ**] On thru Lake Country mountains very impressive with clouds & gloom around them. Went & stood at the gate of Dove Cottage & thought of Dorothy & Wm Wordsworth & pictured Dorothy's quick step and wild glancing Eye as she sped along the path. —Then on to the churchyard to the graves of them all & Quillinan (son in law).[43] On to Haworth up a fearfully steep hill to old church of Patrick Bronte.

[**RJ**] The tirling-pin—"tirling at the pin" in the Scotch ballads. Instead of a knocker, you draw the key (or ring) up and down the twisted iron of the ~~latch~~ handle under the latch. It makes a brave clattering. We saw our first tirling-pin at John Knox's house. Why have they quit using them and taken to knockers?

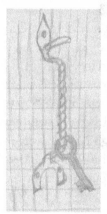

[**DJ**] At Keighley there are buses that looked like common gasoline buses but they are run by electricity from overhead wires like trams. [**RJ**] We arrived after hours at the Bronte parsonage in Haworth, now a museum, but were let in and had the place to ourselves. Una was fascinated and the rest of us at least interested in the thousand tiny manuscripts, the little rooms, and pitiful personal relics. [**UJ**] {Touched by wedding dress of C.B. & a calico one (pink), wedding dress blue with

---

[43] Edward Quillinan, husband of Wordsworth's daughter Dora.

white pinstripe & comb of E.B. half burned. It dropped from her hand to fire when she was so weak at the last & yet sat up to comb her hair. Comb rescued by Tabitha.[44] Saw her dog keepers collar. Lots of manuscripts held one in my hand. — —} [RJ] —But then in the evening we found this Yorkshire factory landscape the grimy streets and blackened walls, and mine-dumps, most awful of tumuli, impossible to escape from. We drove south like people in a nightmare and stopped for supper at the White Swan Hotel in Halifax. After supper we decided to stay the night there. I told the boys they would discover what awfulness the words "Go to Halifax" mean. But instead, they were delighted with the big hotel, and the lift, which they could work themselves by pushing buttons.

UJ Monday, September 23
[RJ] South again next morning, and after hours of driving the country began to be real again. We lingered awhile at Kenilworth Castle, and in the lawns there first fully noticed the drought England has suffered this year, and down south through a country that reminded us of California in autumn. At Stratford we bought cakes and buns and fruit, and came at last in darkness through Moreton-in-the-Marsh to the Unicorn Hotel at Stow-on-the-Wold. There Una was like one imparadised, in the tipsy five-hundred-year old coaching Inn, nothing vertical nothing horizontal, nothing loud nor uncomfortable, and Garth found me a ~~copy~~ little book about the Roll-right Stones, I spent the evening in reading it. While Una wrote letters, and thought of the gilt unicorn on the swinging sign outside our window. The chaste and Grave unicorn.

UJ Tues. Sept 24 1929
[RJ] Next morning we went to see the Rollright Stones, fantastically eroded limestone stone-circle, eight- or nine-foot-

---

[44] Tabitha "Tabby" Aykroyd, beloved servant of the Bronte family.

height. King Stone across the road, north-north-east of the circle—in Warwickshire, the others in Oxfordshire—and the tall cromlech with fallen capstone three hundred yards away. At Keswick I had noticed an erect pillar-stone, though a small one, at a distance outside the circle, as the King Stone is outside this one. At Stonehenge there is the Friar's Heel outside the circles.

It seems to me ridiculous to imagine that these circles were primarily astronomical observatories.

We went on to Britwell-Salome, where our trunks had arrived safely. Una partially [UJ] unpacked the trunks, repacked & took a fresh supply of things to No 7 Lansdowne. —Biddy's place is in quiet peaceful English country not dramatic country but quiet, and near the Cotswolds which are full of beautiful places. {Our arrival here saddened very much by news of death of our dear Jesse Lynch Williams} Came on up to London & found the Barkans[45] had been looking for us at Britwell & were here at the Royal Hotel. Phoebe came out in the evening. — No 7 is a large house with a lovely quiet garden where one forgets one is so near such traffic as we found on the Uxbridge Road. Mrs. O'Sullivan[46] is very kind and eager to make us happy. —She is very clever & amusing and the food delicious & we are glad to be here.

UJ Wed Sept 25   Went in morning with Ellen to Kensington Museum (War Relics) and the Museum of Natural History. Picked up Oddie Barkan on the way. Donnan much thrilled with war relics—amazingly interesting to me—and the Natural History very fine too. Then we went to Royal Palace Hotel & had fine lunch with Barkans. Then boys went to Kensington

---

[45] Dr. Hans Barkan, chairman of the Department of Ophthalmology at Stanford University, and his wife Phoebe, friends of Robinson and Una. The Barkans were traveling with their two children—five-year-old Phoebe and twelve-year-old Adolph ("Adi," pronounced "Oddie").

[46] Bess O'Sullivan, mother of Biddy and sister-in-law of Ellen O'Sullivan.

Park to ~~sail~~ run Oddie's boat (mechanical) Barkans very amusing (so was I) about trials of travelling with children. And Barkan has been ill too. —They were travelling in state with a nurse for children and heaps of luggage and a German cousin (of Hans) actor and studying for his degree Doctor of Philosophy. Hans & Phoebe are dear people I love them & precious children. Phoebe tiny & fragile & quaint & Oddie intelligent & good manners. We went later to No 7 to tea in the garden. Percy called me to ask me to go to Sea Gull that evening but I thought I was too tired. Glad I didn't go as Donnan had eaten too great a selection of hors d'oeuvres & was sick & went to bed without his dinner.

UJ Thurs. Sept 26 Took a walk in morning & to Zoo in P.M. Very hot & dusty & tiring. Enjoyed pelicans & white bears with their tricks & the boys rode an elephant & a camel (both, both) In evening Mrs. Alfred Sutro and her son from San Francisco. Dinner in garden.

UJ Friday Sept 27 To Hemel Hempstead in our car to have lunch with Cary Baynes in Marlowes house. A charming house they have, set in an enormous garden with a stream running through. Cary isn't well, lame with rheumatism & really looks ill. He[47] has gone to work with Jung in Zürich. She is going soon to spend winter. They came to see us in Britwell but of course we were not there. Great yews in the garden & trees of every kind. Gathered hazelnuts. Ximena[48] sweet to boys & they wandered through garden by the brook & climbed a tree & watched the ducks & we all sat on a bench by the water and talked. Cary is a clever & an amusing person with a brilliant mind & such a sense of fun. —We had beef roast & Yorkshire pudding & spotted dog pudding. Very English for our benefit. Back home & hurried dressing. I went to Charlotte St (in the

---

[47] Helton Godwin "Peter" Baynes, Cary's husband.
[48] Ximena was Cary's daughter by her first husband, Jaime de Angulo.

tube) to dine with Percy & Kettle. We had very good dinner with cocktails & wine and wonderful fruit. Saw actors & literary lights Elsa Lanchester & her husband Percy says best actor in London ~~Lawson or Lawton~~ Laughton & Miss — Lehmann author of *Dusty Answer.* I don't know whether I like Percy much or not. He seems a shell.

UJ Sat Sept 28. Boys went to Selfridges with Ellen & other explorings in AM. I wrote letters & sewed etc. In P.M. a lovely drive of 35 miles through sweet Eng country to Roxford, Hertingfordbury, Hert[fordshire] to country house to spend P.M. & tea. It was like a novel read long ago— Mrs Stuart Hogg & her family. Her married daughter. Mrs. Hoggs house old mellow brick of different periods gardens barns—the river Lea running sweetly through the meadow—meadows everywhere—and pheasants— There was a large manor house there at one time and they dig up fragments of carved stone etc. Beneath the level spot where we had tea [GJ] The country just teemed with pheasants and partridges. I saw about a hundred of the former and twenty of the latter. The pheasants were very tame and I could get up to about twenty feet from them. [UJ] There are subterranean cellars which were so dangerous they closed them up. Her daughter & family live in an angel red brick cottage with dormers and surrounded with flowers. Very lovely! Five whole & part sets of twins there. — Everyone going in and out for tea. Cambridge youth & friend came & went into the river. Interesting old barns with fine oak beams & an old cottage fixed up for Mr. Hogg's fisherman friends to meet in. An idyllic afternoon. —

UJ Sat. Sept 28 (insert) How could I have neglected to note down our visit to Madame Toussaud's Wax Works. All my life I had heard of them but never imagined how it would all be. Robin and I went to amuse boys (with disdain!) but were thoroughly entertained. We went at night all brilliantly lit up—room after room with *hundreds* of figures in natural attitudes & apparently *alive*! Kings & queens, writers, adventurers—men politically famous Beautiful Women. —Then below in vaulted cellars in dim light a "Chamber of Horrors" where famous criminals & murderers were, either standing as if at the bar or were depicted in the act of violence. A most amazing place. Thronged with spectators. We went all around twice. In the ticket booth 2 young women twins apparently to receive tickets—We discover one was wax. A policeman who seems to intercept us also a wax image.[49]

UJ Sunday Sept 29 Went to lunch at her[50] club boys & I. Fine old Dartmouth House. Fine oak panelling etc. Quiet and well bred place. Excellent food. Before that we had gone to Catholic Cathedral at Westminster to see it & hear fine choir singing Palestrina one boy sang like a lark. —Then to Buckingham Palace to see the changing of the guards. Very pompous on Sunday fine band. {When we were wandering around near Dartmouth House saw old iron rings to hold torches & big tube shaped pointed end things like candle snuffers to snuff them, by side of entrance.} **[GJ]** Father and I went to the zoo in the afternoon, since it was Sunday nobody but Fellows and people provided with tickets from Fellows could get in. A friend of Mrs O'Sullivan gave us our tickets. The Fireback pheasants were out of their houses and in the yard and looked much bigger than I expected. We discovered several new pens of animals that we hadn't seen before. Two aviaries of lapwings, snipe, quail, hornbills and little birds. Also a house with two goats and a baby rhino in it. Its funny how those two always seem to go together. Saw an aviary of peacocks and lots of elk and sambur and red deer. Also saw a place called the

---

[49] In order to incorporate this insert, Una pasted it over the original September 28th entry and rewrote the original entry on the next two pages, on the second of which Garth had already written his entry about the pheasants.

[50] Ellen O'Sullivan.

monkey hill. It was a big pit with a pile of concrete in the middle in it were about 50 baboons. The old males kept running amuck and racing around barking and growling until another one made a dash at them when they would turn tail and run. We saw the chimpanzees having tea, they were very human and drank their tea and ate their fruit as well as human children one tried to pass the keeper a grape but he refused. We went into the parrot house and the noise almost split our heads I let a macaw take my finger in its mouth and when I remarked how nice its tongue felt it stuck its own fingers in its mouth to see. [UJ] Percy came for supper. Donnan & I had gone to the Victoria & Albert Museum. Saw fine wood-carvings, tapestries & mosaics etc. Rained hard for an hour.

RJ Monday Sept 30 We drove out to Windsor, through the extraordinary traffic of Shepherd's Bush, and over the Kew Bridge. And several other bridges, through Richmond, Kingston and Staines. At Kingston a fine old rambling half-timbered brick house being scraped and repaired. Una and the boys ran back a block to look at it. Between Staines and Windsor the twisting pleasant Thames, with lawn on this side and willow thickets on the other, and eight or ten big swans between. We stopped for picnic lunch, the swans clambered from the water and bullied us out of our biscuits. Their heads at a stretch were nearly as high as the boys' or Una's. We looked for notches on their beaks (the swan-upping story*) but found none. At Windsor the great pretentious castle, the Queen's doll's house, quite amusing, the state apartments, intolerable gilt furniture, cockney-speaking guide, Holbeins of little interest, Vandykes of none, ridiculous painted ceilings, 777 escutcheons of Knights of the Garter. Oh, England! But Donnan had at last seen a furnished castle, and was much pleased. We bought some dry buns in the town to stuff the Thames swans on the way back, and fed them until they swam away. Home by the Staines Road and the Great West Road.

It seems to me curious that everything we have seen so far in England is second-rate. The country of course is sick with drought; but London especially, an enormous aggregation of second-rate and second-rate, spread very thin. I'm sorry that I have no liking for England. The people are decent and good-natured, and a little pitiful, going down in the world; but there is nothing hitherto to interest me, south of Westmoreland, in the earth or the air. The soft subdued earth or the helpless serene air. All stale and familiar and spiritless; occasionally a little quaint.

* The story about "upping the swans" is amusing. On a certain day each year three barges set forth from London up the Thames. They fly broad banners, and the oarsmen wear scarlet coats. Year by year it is a longer journey to where the swans can be found, as London spreads up the river, but the place of embarkation must not be changed. They catch the swans and notch their bills, one third are marked for the King, one third for the Vintners' Guild, one third for the Dyers' Guild. The swans are marked and set free, and that is all. Of course no one ever wants them for anything, except to be ornaments of the Thames, which they were already. Una repeated this story to her old friend Kettle. He saw nothing amusing in it. He knew about the practice; and of course they had to be marked, so that they might be tame swans instead of mere wild ones.

Yes, that is characteristic of this poor English earth; it has had its bill notched, very thoroughly, for most of 2000 years. I think that's its charm for its lovers; they like to finger the notches.

[UJ] {Apropos of queer clauses in leases & deeds. Mrs O' S held her title with freedom to use any way except to "keep a pig or make soap."}

UJ Tues Oct 1

[RJ] I went with the boys, Donnan's second visit to the Imperial War Museum, which fascinates him. Una stopped off on the way to do our banking, and later rejoined us. An attendant noticed Donnan's interest, and talked to him at length. The man spoke cheerfully of the next war, and hoped he would be employed in a munitions factory again. He was not a hypocrite; I believe most of the non-combatants, and ~~many~~ some of the soldiers, enjoyed the war more than anything before or since. They trod their peaks then. But England cannot afford the luxury of another. Air-power has nullified England's old security, that seems to me the great political fact of modern times, and relatively to the rest of the world she must go down and down.

UJ Wed Oct 2 To British Museum with Ellen very interesting. As always I liked best the sculpture. We all were interested in mummies. The man in the gem room showed us the only unicorn among the 4000 intaglios. It was 2000 BC & was head only head of unicorn backed up against head of man— symbolic. Saw Museum ghost a queer reflection into a stone coffin. In P.M. went to Peter Steffens mothers for tea. She is typically Jewish but very nice. German accent slight resemblance to Peter. Young Pete naughty broke toys and hit boys. Swiss nurse. Evening with Ellen & Bess to Apple Cart by Shaw.[51] I do not like Shaw & the second act was intolerable. Voices with one exception very poor. Audience loved the play. Chief theme seemed to be to show the necessity of keeping the king for figurehead.

UJ Thurs Oct 3 Robin boys & I to tower. We went across London Bridge & walked back. Went all over Tower—crown jewels, Traitors Gate, room of murdered princes & execution block, armor etc. Then walked along Fleet St. Saw St. Pauls. —Went to Old Cheshire Cheese too late for lunch. Got good cheap lunch at ABC. Mrs & Mr (son) Chisholm dined here. We walked thru Temple cloisters & little streets saw Pump Court & Fountain Court etc. Evening Ellen took boys & Biddy & me to Murder on the Second Floor very amusing detective story.

---

[51] George Bernard Shaw.

UJ Friday Oct 4 Went to Aylesford near Maidstone to see Kit's
Coty House the biggest cromlech yet seen the sideblocks
enormous sandstone. In a field nearby the Countless Stones
also of ancient origin—possible a cromlech or two fallen
down. Very lovely old village is Aylesford. Very bad traffic. To
Matriarch[52] (Mrs. Pat Campbell) with Ellen. Very fine—*strong*
Jewish family ties—theme. Home on top of bus.

UJ Sat, October 5 To nice Eng dentist in morning. Donnan & I
must both have a filling. Then downtown to Selfridges—then
to Houses of Parliament (*fine* Westminster Hall) then to Abbey.
Oh it is inspiring—the proportion & the carved stone & wood
& the exquisite stained glass & the great space in spite the
crowding tombs. Saw the wax effigies for the first time. Only
about 12 of them in tiny stone upper closet. Wax effigies made
& carried in funeral procession of deceased. Often made from
death masks. In their own clothes. Charles II very dark & sad
in costume worn at some Garter function 3 days before his
death. Stood beside Thomas Hardy's tablet let into floor above
his ashes & beside Grave of Unknown Soldier. Took boys
around the beautiful cloisters & pointed out to them that sad
& touching tablet in the wall

> Jane Lister
> dear childe
> died Oct 7, 1688
> > {1929 – 1688   241 yrs ago}

{Sat P.M. Went to fine cinema Four Feathers made by the
man[53] who did "Grass." Boys love escalators.}
Susan & Valentine came for dinner.[54] Susan very entertaining
& Valentine handsome. The Lindsay plaids I ordered for

---

52 A play by Gladys Bronwyn Stern.
53 Merian C. Cooper, screenwriter and director.
54 Susan Creighton (Williams) Porter, actress and storyteller active in the
Carmel theater community, and her daughter Valentine.

Mamma & me from Inverness came very nice. {"I am the only Running Footman" Inn. Unicorn seal—}

UJ Sunday [October 6] To lunch with Ellen at her club again boys & I. Excellent lunch again. Then for an hour through National Gallery and a look at the Lions in Trafalgar Square. Then back to No 7. High wind & leaves swirling   a few riders in Rotten Row. Picked up Robin & we drove along the Embankment, along Grovenor Road. Thames all whipped up, waves running high and the river boats rolling. The row of sycamore trees with bare trunks and leaves falling a fine sight against the gray water. Went past fine old houses "Old Swan House" "The Clock House" etc. —Then turned up Cheyne Walk. Got out & stood awhile looking at Carlyle's house and thought about his life there. Home then meandering along the Embankment and over the Putney Bridge (& back again!) via Shepherd's Bush. Julie Heineman's sister for dinner, then later Miss Hall authority in ~~Irish antiquities~~ no! Gaelic language. Very amusing but I did not get any real information out of her.
("The House of Confinement" cut in lintel of little blind stone house roofed with enormous stone slabs (near Alfreton))[55]
She was a pupil of Kuno Meyer the great Gaelic scholar. She has written a Gaelic dictionary. Was bitter because Meyer lectured against England in the World War.

UJ Monday Oct 7 In morning shopping with Ellen after a brief visit to dentist. We spent a long time at Libertys   bought a few things. Went looking for amber. Its gotten very expensive. We saw St. George chase the dragon and stab him in the clock outside Libertys. Went to Yardley's beautiful shop. Ellen gave

---

[55] This interruption, written in pencil in an entry otherwise written in ink, was written earlier when the Jefferses were traveling to London from Scotland. Alfreton is a village in Derbyshire, in the central part of England. Una put parentheses in ink around this sentence when she encountered it later.

me some powder from there. Went to Selfridges. She gave me
a wonderful lunch kit for four to carry in automobile. Home.
In P.M. we (Robin and I) drove to Tavistock Square to tea with
Virginia & Leonard Woolf. A big old fashioned house. Their
Hogarth Press is beneath the house in the big *old* wine cellars.
Very fine sensitive faces both of them and interesting. She
pleased *me* by admiring George Moore tremendously. She said
that her frozen *Thames* happened to have occurred actually
about the date of her story in Orlando. They were very friendly
& he toasted muffins for us by the fire. We enjoyed our time
with them. They advise us to go to Zennor, Cornwall for the
winter. Promised to write to a friend there about a house for
us. Back through crowded traffic & glare of lamps to No 7.
{Boys had had a fine walk with Bess & Mr Pincher (Biddy's
police dog) in the park.} Susan Porter had left with Ellen for
us to read a long letter from Tyrell Williams all about Jesse's
death. He died at the home of the Douglass Robinsons his dear
friends (Mrs D R a sister of Theodore Roosevelt). A gay party
there including Archie Roosevelt. Alice had gone upstairs to
rest. Jesse was talking to the others & reached forward for a
cigarette—gasped fell back unconscious and was dead in
twenty minutes. —a stroke. He and Alice & Laidlaw had been
up to the island off the Maine Coast where their summer home
was, then motoring through New England.

UJ Tues. Oct 8. Packed in morning. Donnan briefly to dentist. A
pelting rain. We drove out to Kerry Vor Oxfordshire in the
downpour. Looked dreary when we arrived. Biddy & Valentine
just going. In evening to "The Rest." Good dinner with Hans
& Phoebe Barkan.

UJ Wed Oct 9. Settling. The maid Mrs. Newell very nice & good
cook. The big kitchen sitting room with great fireplace & big
dresser filled with gay china, the red brick floor & comfortable
chairs make a charming room. Boys to "The Rest" to play &
have lunch. In PM Barkans came & we motored to Ewelme the

most beautiful little village with a fine old church and picturesque almshouses adjoining. All faded red brick with black timbering. Red ivy (autumnal coloring) over the walls & sweet little gardens. Phoebe & I drove back. Husbands & sons walked picking blackberries by the way. Brought us a big bowlful. In morning we had driven to Oxford taking Oddie; much red tape to get check cashed.

UJ Thursday Oct 10. Drove up to London via Henley. Drove to Crystal Palace to tremendous dog show over 2500 dogs. Fine mastiffs & bulldogs & Irish wolfhounds. Bloodhounds not so fine as I have seen in USA. Through awful traffic to center of London to go to Prince of Wales Theatre in Haymarket. Got off our road again & again. Traffic dreadful. At last in the thickest part of town *The Strand* got out & left car parked by St. Clement Danes Robin in it with book—boys & I took tube at Temple Station. Late for play but saw enough of it. It lasted until 5:30. Not awfully good. All played in dark dugout. One gets tired of the dimness & sameness. Voices & enunciation poor. Boys thrilled. Scuttled back to Robin and then for hours it seemed drove through most awful traffic jam I ever saw—along Oxford Street, Uxbridge Road etc. Arrived home in light rain at 8:00. Soon Ella Winter came with her friend Ena Mitrany writer & wife of a Roumanian. They live at Kingston Blount five miles away. Ena fair—golden hair—nice person. Peter goes home Oct 16. —Took them all over house with candle. They have been motoring in Dorset.

UJ Friday Oct 11. Took boys to "The Rest" for lunch. In P.M. went ourselves there to tea. Grand tea. Home & read. Wild bird calls in evening. We begin to feel very contented here.

UJ Sat Oct 12. Took Barkans to Oxford with us. Completed cashing check! Nice ride. All PM Robin signed the sheets for special autographed edition of "Dear Judas." Late before supper drove into Watlington for supplies. Very quaint houses about here with sweet gardens. This garden is strewn with yew berries now. {A saying "Pereant qui ante nos nostra dixerunt"}[56]

DJ Sun. Oct. [13] Spent day making "rickshaw" with pair of old pram wheels. We started copying this diary in a "round tower" notebook we got in ~~Donegal~~ {Drogheda}.[57] Barkans came for tea. We took turns with "Oddy" pulling each other; two of us would pull while we took the other one for a spin. The one who was going to ride would say "Ease it down—Stand up—Stand at attention—Turn it around—Whoa—Slow walk—Trot!—Gallop!" and then after a while "Slow down—Whoa—Ease it down—Help me up—I now have the honor to give Sir Oddy Barkan the whip" (with wich we beat our slaves). Oddy would say "Thank you, your honor" and then when he got the whip, "Get in there you brutes, hannis up" and then we would start off again. [**UJ**] Walked almost to "Rest" with Barkans. Soft quiet air a moon through thin clouds. All still—a few night birds.

UJ Monday Oct [14] Barkans hired car & driver & we all set out in the two cars for days trip after Robin & I had had wild time getting sheets for *Dear Judas* off. Had to stamp with our special unicorn seal 17 times. We went through Ewelme Dorchester Abingdon etc to Wantage (home of Hardys "Jude"), then through White Horse Vale visited "Blowing Stone" which King Alfred was said to have used to call his armies together. When one blew thru a hole in top a great blast like a trumpet came forth (or a bellowing bull). It stands about 4 ft high under a tree with a hinged board clamped over hole. One must pay to have it unlocked & be allowed to blow. Then on to White Horse a strange chalk figure (turf cut away, exposing chalk underneath) high hill 900 ft. elev.   image over 1000 yrs. old.

---

[56] "May they perish who said first what we were going to say."
[57] Added by Una.

Air fine and bracing up there. It is said one can see into 11 counties from top. A Roman camp on top and pre-Roman deep (dry) moat around central raised place. Below is an artificial (?) hill where St. George is said to have slain the dragon. Ate lunch on hill had fine sherry Hans gave us yesterday. Then on to Lechlade & Kelmscott Manor. Mae Morris lives there. She allows people to see it (for a compensation) proceeds go to building village hall in honor of Wm Morris. Saw so many things I knew about. Tapestries, oak table, loom, chairs, pictures by Rossetti & Burne Jones, Icelandic horns (carved) etc.

> "Kelmscott Manor, the old gabled house, **[GJ]** and the garden with its hollyhocks and clipped yew hedge, {said Wm Morris}[58] has come to me to be the type of the pleasant places of the earth, and of the homes of harmless simple people, not overburdened with the intricacies of life; and as others love the race of man through their lovers or their children, so I love the earth through that small space of it."

Saw Morris' bound *MSS* of *Sundering Flood* and *Well at World's End*. Saw a Kelmscott Chaucer. It lay in middle of that great black oak bed for which Morris wrote those verses & May Morris embroidered on top valance. "The ~~winds~~ snows on the wold, the winds acold." Saw many portraits of Mrs Morris. — *Old* tapestries very lovely completely covered walls of one room. —Episodes in Life of Samson. Door cut right *through* tapestry. These were there when Morris bought the Manor fine carved stone fireplaces. A pair of virginals in case on table. She said very fine ones but no one, not even Dolmetsch,[59] can keep them in tune **[RJ]** here. In London they were always in tune. **[UJ]** {She was pleased when boys commented on a series of Dürer drawings on wall in the passage.} Walked in garden lovely garden old apple trees & yews & flowers & fruit against

---

[58] Added by Una.
[59] Eugène Arnold Dolmetsch, French-born musician and instrument maker.

the walls & box hedge. {fine topiary work (cf Sigurd's Dragon)} Beautiful mellow stone, gabled house. Small square paned windows, barns group finely. High wall (10 ft perhaps) all about garden. Dovecot. {Miss Morris asked us many questions about California. She was much interested in my "Cairngorm" wine. She was about to make grape wine. She was *exceedingly* interested in my cream colored homespun dress from Connemara.} We gave her £2 toward memorial. Old Oxfordshire houses beautiful much red brick mellowed. Now the Boston ivy red as blood beautiful against the walls of red. Forest trees turning to yellow & red. Air full of dancing leaves. Many flocks of lovely sheep in picturesque moveable wooden fences (hurdles) many snub nose houses like ours {Tor House}.

At Wantage a statue of Alfred the Great by Count Gleichen[60]

> "Alfred the Great
> The West Saxon King
> born at Wantage A.D. 849.
> Alfred found learning dead
> And he restored it.
> Education neglected
> And he revived it.
> The laws powerless
> And he gave them force
> The Church debased
> And he raised it
> The land ravaged by a fearful enemy
> from which he delivered it.
> Alfred's name will live as long as
> mankind shall respect the past . . ."

The haystacks here are often shaped like houses with roofs sometimes snub-nosed & *thatched*. I almost cried on the way home when the light failed it had been so beautiful. Heard a skylark on top White Horse Hill.

---

[60] Count Albert Edward Wilfred Gleichen.

Throughout our trip the boys would transform themselves into
the most hideous creatures as they undressed for bed, called
"cootie hunters" (after some character in a war story) and peer
& slink about the bedrooms until we were weak with laughter.

Inns[61]

~~Ye Ancient Grudge~~

~~Eagle & Childe (Staveley)~~

Whoop Hall—(near Settle)

Unicorn Hotel (Shipton)

Ring O' Bells Inn (Kendal)

Wheat Sheaf   "   "

Grey Bull   " (Penrith)

Hope & Anchor "

  (Keighley)

Horseshoe Hotel (Ripley)

Thorn Tree   "   "

The Old Bell & Harp (near

  Derby)

Castle & Falcon (Derby)

Hay Inn

Wheel Inn (near Ashby)

Globe Inn (")

Shoulder of Mutton Inn

         (Ashby)

The Fox and Hounds (")

Black Horse (Sheepy

  Magna)

[ ] Three [ ] (Atherson)

[ ] Swan Inn (")

~~The Five Alls~~ (by

  Dashwood Hill)

The Load of Mischief

The Blue Boar

  (Atherson)

Half Moon Inn

        (Nuneaton)

Ye Olde Wharfe [Inn] (")

Beehive Inn (Bedworth)

Rising Sun   (")

Engine Inn (near Coventry)

Grouse Inn (Coventry)

Virgins Inn & Castle

Tavern (Kenilworth)

The Porridge Pot ([ ])

~~Eagle & Childe~~

~~The Lamb & Flag~~

The Rifle But

The Old Angel

  (Buckingham)

Ye Old White Bear

  (Shipston-on-Stour)

The Dumb Bell Hotel

The Five Alls

The Three Magpies

The Pond House

Running Horse Inn—

  Mickleham

Maid's Head Norwich

---

[61] The list of Inns that follows was written on the last pages of the first
notebook devoted to this diary. Presumably the family added to it as they
traveled.

Saracen's Head—
  Dartmoor
Ye Old Fighting Cocks
  St. Albans
The Anchor Petersfield
The Dolphin [Petersfield]
Crown & Angel Norwich
Blue Eyed Maid London
2 Puddings [London]
Jollie Butchers [London]
Hand & Shears [London]
Swan with 2 Necks
  [London]
Punch Bowl & Ladle
  [London]
Druid's Head (near
  Salisbury)
Leather Bottle
Baldfaced Stag
  Roehampton
St Peter's Finger
  Lytchett Minster Dorset
Eagle & Child—Alderley
  Edge Cheshire
Ship & Turtle—Grove
  Mill
{The 3 Loggerheads
  We 3 Loggerheads be}
Ye Old Spotted Dog
Old Welsh Harp
Upper Welsh Harp
~~Bald Faced Stag~~
~~The Bee Hive~~
The Windmill
The Foresters Arms
  (Bushy)
The Merry Month of May
  (")

The Leather Sellers Arms
The Fishmongers   "
Eight Bells (Watford)
Swan & Pyramids
The Whip & Collar
  (Hemel Hempstead)
The Case is Altered
The Woodman
The New Fiddle (Hatfield)
The Boar & Castle (")
The White Black Bird
Old Roebuck
Rose of Lee
Recent Fish Restaurant
Ye Old Robin Hood
The Green Man (Potters
  Bar)
~~Ye Old Robin Hood~~
The Bull & Butcher
  Finchley
The Hand & Flower
  [Finchley]
The Three Horseshoes
  [Finchley]
~~The Swan with Two~~
  ~~Necks~~ [Finchley]
The Gray Nag
Bird in Hand
The Barley Mow
  (Watlington)
Sun in Splendor
The French Horn
The One Bell
The Arab Boy
The Kentish Yeoman
The Walnut Tree
Dog & Fox
The Spotted Cow

The Horse & Groom
Old Tiger's Head
The Cab Tree
{The Swan and Bottle
(near West Wycombe)}
Ye Ancient Grudge—
Tewkesbury
The Running Footman—
London (**Sign** I am the
only Running Footman)
Hark! The Lasher!
The Crossed Hands
near Stow-in-the-Wold
Glou[cestershire]
" Hampshire Hog
(London)
" Packhorse and Talbot
(")
" ~~Sun In Splendour (")~~
" Blue Anchor
(Richmond)
" Old Ship   (")
" Compasses   (")
" Pigeon   (")
" Star and Garter (")
" Fox & Duck (near ")
" British Oak (Kingston)
" Crown & Thistle (")
" Grey Horse   (")
" Old King's Head (")
" ~~Running Horse~~

———— ~~(Sunbury)~~
" Shears (")
~~" Jolly Butcher (Slanes)~~
" North Star   (")
Ye Bells of Ouzeley
Stag & Hounds
Jolly Waggoners
Master Robert
Gardeners Arms (London)
Bricklayers Arms   (")
Ginger Cat Café
~~Swan & Bottle~~
Gravel Diggers Arms
Friend at Hand
The Lamb and Flag Hotel
(*Oxford*)
~~The Case is Altered~~
~~(Harrow Weald)~~
The Farmer's Man
(Benson)
The Jolly Ploughboy
Abingdon
The Old Air Balloon Inn
(Wantage)
Ye Old Post-Office Vaults
Ye Old Trout Inn
(Lech[ ])
The Folly (Faringdon)
Crown and Trumpet
(Broad [ ])
The Bold Venture

UJ Tuesday Oct 15. At home all morning mending etc. Mrs. Newell the "help" is making us very comfortable. "Oddy" Barkan came to play with boys. Went to say goodbye to Barkans who go to London today. In P.M. we went to Watlington for supplies then to the beautiful village of Ewelme {*ū-elm pronounced*} to buy some postcards. A wonderful old church there and old almshouses & quaint groups of dwellings along the twisty street. Then slowly back through the gray light through Brightwell & Upperton & Cuxham back through Watlington to Kerry Vor. Peter Steffens sails tomorrow, Barkans a week from today.

UJ Wed Oct 16. —All day trip. First to Bank Oxford & have car greased—then to Broadway, the beautiful Cotswold village so much photographed home of Mary Anderson (Madam De Navarro). On to Willersey where we could rent Miss Huntington's friends' house. All sweet villages here gray & yellow stone. Went through Moreton-in-the-Marsh & Stow-on-the-Wold (where we had stayed one night at Unicorn Hotel). On through Bibury which Wm Morris called "the most beautiful village in England." It *is*. Lovely gray houses up & down a hilly street & beside a clear sweet little river with swans on it which winds & twists under old stone bridges— on again through Kelmscott where we wished to see Morris' grave but the church was locked. Back through early evening home. A great full moon looked down. We remembered last full moon the harvest moon. We drove beside Loch Lomond home from Tarbert to Uplawmoor. Our headlights went out & we were lucky to have the moon.

UJ Thurs. Oct 17. Home all day. Boys & I have bad colds. Garth caught it somewhere. In PM a charming drive. Went up the hill beyond Watlington & through Northend etc—way around to Henley & back. Thames beautiful near Henley. Woods beautiful above where we were —great forests of beech & elm etc (a few white birch) all turned red & yellow & pink. Such ancient old red brick farm houses. Left our passport & Eng registration books with police at Watlington. Woman there wringing her hands & saying "We're having trouble at Windmill Farm."

UJ Friday ~~Sept~~ Oct 18. Home in morn & letters. In P.M. Robin washed car. We walked in the late P.M. across a wide field of stubble. At one end men were thrashing. We walked toward them but they stopped before we reached them. Air nippy with frost. Walked along a deep lane between high trees. Picked some crabapples. Just as puckery as when I was a child. Walked past a farm house had a gravestone in one corner of yard. (Mrs. N says its the old graveyard & an old owner of the farm lies there). Garth sees many pheasants & hares. Mrs. N tells him how the hares wrestle in the fields. Moonlight. While we walk we eat hazelnuts we have filled our pockets with.

UJ Saturday ~~Sept~~ Oct 19. After shopping home until late P.M. More letters. Took a brief fast walk. Stopped to feed some apples to a herd of pretty Jersey cows who raced along the other side the hedge beside us. Boys and I (Robin at last moment refused to go) went to motion picture in a weird little cinema house to see "The Legion of the ~~Damned~~ Condemned." Companion picture to "Wings." Not nearly as fine as Wings but good. A most unprepossessing lot of young men at the show. Bought 1/ of the delicious Watlington cream & we sat down and ate it at supper on applesauce. Hot Ovaltine after show. Ellen O'S telephoned after we were gone tonight. Frosty.

UJ Sunday ~~Sept~~ Oct 20. Baked beans & made crust for meat pie. Letters. Hard rain all day. Late we walked a brisk mile and then had to change our clothes when we came back although we'd worn our raincoats. Robin read "Precious Bane"[62] aloud. Garth worked with modelling today. Donnan drew. Police arrived before breakfast with our passports etc. Glad to get them back.

UJ Monday ~~Sept~~ Oct 21 We walked in late P.M. to Brightwell and then back across a field by a footpath to Britwell. Late red sun,

---

[62] A novel by Mary Webb.

frosty air. We gathered some blackberries very ripe & sweet and gazed upon the beautiful berries in hedges, bright red hips, maroon haws, orange red rowan, dark blue sloe & elderberries, brilliant scarlet holly. —The autumn trees are beautifully colored orange yellow & red. These Oxfordshire houses of mellow red brick with thatch or flat red tile roofs are very lovely and the buildings beautifully grouped. [**RJ**] Written on the gate of a cottage in Cuxham—name of the place or what? —"Ancient Lights." [**UJ**] Name over a store here in Watlington *Thirza Appleby*. {Lovegrove is name of Bakery}

UJ Tues. Oct 22. Started on trip. Went to Stratford-on-Avon first. Visited Shakespeares Birth Place & garden New Place & Museum, church with his grave & tablets (interested in the church register with his birth & death notices). Went to Shottery & through Anne Hathaways house. —Drove on to Warwick. Stopped at Woolpack Arms where Bert Gearing[63] & I stayed a night or two in 1912. We had a lovely big room with 3 beds & all lovely old mahogany furniture. A fireplace & we had a good fire all evening & wine as usual & Eng magazines.

UJ Wed ~~Sept~~ Oct 23. Warwick Castle. Peacocks in garden. Magnificent cedars of Lebanon "smoking" pollen blown off. Fine castle—the very flower of English castles— Cedar panelled room fine— fine armor, pathetic small armor for the "noble impe" (one leg of armor shorter than other) a young deformed scion of the house buried in Warwick Church. Lovely table inlaid with lapis lazuli cornelian etc. Strange wild hunted portrait of Strafford[64] after his long trial—just before execution. Cromwell's[65] dented helmet & death mask. Extraordinarily fine tapestries of XVI cent. French finest *detail*

---

[63] Alberta Gearing, an acquaintance Una traveled with briefly on her 1912 trip abroad.
[64] Thomas Wentworth, 1st Earl of Strafford, Lord Deputy of Ireland.
[65] Oliver Cromwell.

of any tapestries in England. Great vase from Hadrian's villa in garden. Our route—Britwell, Wallington, Cuxham, Oxford, Woodstock, Enstone, Long Compton, Shipston, Stratford-on-Avon, Shottery, Stratford, Warwick, Leamington, Southam, Banbury, Sulgrave, Buckingham, Whitchurch, Aylesbury, Wendover, Great Kimble, Monks Risborough, Princes' Risborough, Missenden, Aston Rowant, Watlington. (Percy & I walked all one day about country around Wendover in 1912) Went around by Sulgrave Manor. Visited thrilling old house opposite now antique shop. —Saw in it a green ball like one the Postmistress gave us at Knocknacarry. Price £1-5/

UJ Thurs. Oct 24. Ellen came at 10:36. Hard rain all day. Shopped then went to old house owned by Speed[66] the artist. Then a walk up a lane in rain toward Ewelme. In P.M. ride to Cuxham. Brightwell, Dorchester (stopped & went into beautiful little church where Ellen goes to mass). On to Ewelme. Tried in vain to buy watercress. Too rainy. Men wouldn't pick any. Home in rain. Hot chocolate for supper with whipped cream on top.

DJ Fri. Oct. 25 Went on lovely walk with Ellen {& Kooch.[67]} — Shortcut to Ewelme. There were many kinds of berries in the hedges. We saw ~~Ewelme~~ house {Britwell House "staring at its monument"} a nice brick manor house with a tall monument commerating some battle in front of it. We each had our pockets full of apples and pears and fed all the horses and cows along the way. {Horses ploughing}. We got two bunches of watercress at Ewelme. {They must supply half of England by the size of the beds.}[68] In the afternoon we took Ellen to the train. We went up a little by-road which after half a mile petered out into a private drive. On both sides of the road there

---

[66] Harold Speed.
[67] The dog belonging to Mrs. Newell.
[68] All bracketed material in this entry added by Una.

were pheasants rabbits and partridges. **[GJ]** Then we went back and did some shopping in Watlington. **[DJ]** Then we went up another byway, wandered around for a while and came home by Nettlebed. About a mile from home one of our tyres went flat. **[UJ]** Sharp flint. Fine clouds. Hedges very beautiful. Bright red hips, dull maroon haws, brilliant scarlet holly & wild plum & orange red rowan berries & blackberries & sloe & elderberries and everywhere gorgeously colored leaves. {When there is an overplentiful supply of berries it is thought to presage a hard winter.} On the way to Ewelme we saw a beautiful old farm once worked by Mrs. Newell's people. She was born there. They are now in the wonderful alms houses at Ewelme.

UJ Saturday, Oct 26. Sewed & wrote letters. Robin took tire down to be fixed. Nothing eventful. Very cold. Robin declaims hatred of Oxfordshire. Started to walk. Went across 2 stubble fields because roads so closed in & dull. —in twilight. Farmer yelled to us to get out. Said we scared the game. We told him nothing there but lapwings. We were as disagreeable as possible. Miserable little object! He is the small farmer Mrs. Newell told us about that is so disagreeable. Washed Garth's hair.

UJ Sunday Oct 27. Rose to find brilliant sunshine but thin coat of ice all across end of duck pond. Boys were happy there all morning shepherding the ducks there & dredging the pond. I got ready the boys new trousers to their suits (knickerbockers too full & long) and took to village tailor (the postman who comes at 6:13 A.M.) to stitch. Fine beef steaks & baked potatoes & onions for dinner. In PM a long walk. We started on the lane to Ewelme, then branched off & went along the Icknield Way (strewn with beechnuts & horse chestnuts) fine beech wood. Then turned, at the crossroads the way opposite to Ewelme. Walked *and* walked crisp afternoon air. Smoky look to distant hills. Gorgeously colored forest trees—

underneath ground looks red ~~with~~ because of fallen leaves. On a stubble field saw portable chicken houses on wagons can be drawn by horses. Hundreds of chickens scratching busily. A half hundred bicyclists pedalled wearily by us up a hill littered with sharp flints. Saw Silene (bladder campion) along road. Surprised. This is the plant the McDuffies[69] gathered in Tintagel Cornwall & gave us for Tor House. Were lost. Directions very hard. Went through Cookley. Went through private roads. At last (after asking farmer from house where loud cries & songs were ringing out) found ourselves on steep hill road running down to Britwell. We once went to Henley that way. A walk of at least 7 miles. Boys went & bought extra qt milk. Made hot chocolate. Blobs of cream on top. Robin finished reading "Precious Bane" aloud. Washed Donnan's hair.

UJ Monday Oct 28. Nothing important. Rain. Letters. Made a fine mince pie & black currant tarts. My shoes to cobbler. Poor Mrs. Rivett's face terribly swollen. 5 teeth out Sat at Oxford infirmary. Robin reads aloud "Widdicombe Fair."[70] A crushed heart-broken letter from Alice Williams. She & boys to stay at Princeton for winter if boys can stand climate. Letter from Percy in P.M.

UJ Tuesday Oct 29. —In PM went to Marlow just beyond Henley to see the house where Shelley[71] lived once. A low 2½ story house set on the street with garden behind. The opposite side of the street has a high wall which hides the Thames from Shelley's house. One wonders how much he could see from his windows. It isn't inspiring country. Over the house is a large

---

[69] Duncan and Jean (Howard) McDuffie were Carmel neighbors. Duncan was an architect and well-known conservationist; Jean, a founder and president of Children's Hospital in Oakland.

[70] *Widecombe Fair*, a novel by Eden Phillpotts.

[71] Percy Bysshe Shelley.

marble tablet put up by Sir — and on it it says that the house
was the abode of Shelley 1816–1817 and that he was visited
here by Byron—there follows a few lines from Adonais. I
doubt Byron's visit. I think they were not ~~great~~ very friendly
before the encounter along with Clare[72] in Switzerland. The
house is now divided into 4 small houses one of which was
empty. We peered into a room through a low window & saw a
very low dark room with a minute fireplace. Of course the
rooms may have been altered & cut up since Shelley's time.
This Oxfordshire country makes one feel shut in and
smothered. I am afraid I shall never like trees so well again.
They are too thick here.

UJ Wednesday Oct 30. One of the things at the Bodleian Library
[DJ] an Egyptian schoolboy's letter of the 2nd or 3rd century A.D.

> Theon to his father Theon. Greeting. It was a fine thing of you
> not to take me with you to town. If you won't take me with you
> to Alexandria, I won't write you a letter or speak to you . . . .
> Mother said to Archelaus, "He upsets me. Take him away." So
> send for me, I implore you. If you won't send, I won't eat, I
> won't drink; there now! Farewell.
> (Endorsed) Deliver to Theon from his son Theon.
>   (dated) Tubi 18

[UJ] We went to Oxford to get repaired the left fenders I
crumpled near John O'Groats against a stone wall when I
swerved because I was gazing on a pillar stone in a field.
{Insurance co paid bill} While it was being fixed Robin & boys
got hairs cut. I shopped. Then we went to the Bodleian Library.
Saw very beautiful illuminated books there, —Tennyson[73] &
Hardy MSS. Death mask of Napoleon. Chair made from wood
taken from Francis Drake's Golden Hinde tiny locket book
about size of thumbnail and the Shelley relics. The Sophocles
drowned with him, his thumb print in the leaves as it was at

---

[72] Claire Clairmont, Mary Shelley's stepsister.
[73] Alfred, Lord Tennyson.

the end his watch stopped at 5:15. On chain 5 seals of his &
Mary's his golden baby rattle with long coral piece to cut teeth
on and a whistle at one end. A locket with his & Mary's hair in
it, a picture of him as a boy & one of Edward Williams as a
boy. Also Williams' watch given to Jane[74] just before they
started on that last fatal voyage; the guitar given by Shelley to
Jane & the MSS. poem he wrote to accompany the gift. On the
stairway are portraits of (2 of) Shelley, Jane, Flora McDonald.
—In the gallery a large portrait of the present Pope.[75] He was
once a Reader at the Bod. When he became Pope the present
Readers sent him an illuminated address. He responded by
sending his portrait. No other visitors in the gallery when we
were there and curator very agreeable & attentive so
remembering Sara Bard Field's tale of the mysterious Shelley
MSS. I said tentatively "Do you happen to know anything
about a Shelley MSS. deposited here some years ago to be
opened in 1922 and made available to the public?" He was up
like a shot & giving me a curious look said "I will get the man
in charge of it to talk to you." —He came, a nice dark youngish
man. "Yes there is such a manuscript. I happen to have edited
it." —"O" said I "then where can I get a copy?" — "Well as a
matter of fact there were no startling revelations or new facts
brought to light—it was purely personal correspondence & the
gist of it is appearing in the Works of Sh— now being edited
with notes and so on by Peck & Ingpen." "Can the public
inspect it? I understood it was to be open to the public." "No
—of course by taking certain steps and upon the
recommendation of certain authorities, it might be possible to
obtain permission to see it. We have been requested not to
show it." "My friend was told that it was being inspected &
edited by someone in London." "Your friend was
misinformed. It has never been out of the Bod. since placed
here. {in 1894 (I think)} I have charge of it." I felt I could not

---

[74] Jane (Cleveland) Williams.
[75] Pius XI.

press the thing further. Indeed he was so courteous and pleasant that I didn't realize until after he was gone how evasive & mysterious he was.

—— ——   —— ——

It was curious to meditate over those Shelley relics—that Sophocles clasped in his hand shoved into his pocket as if for a moment, —to be taken out again when the squall was past— how it went down to the depths with him—and floated clasped in his hand for days in what awful unknown regions in the sea—until he was washed up at Via Reggio and there cremated—but it remained. —Things are *queer*—they make me shiver sometimes their patience & endurance. They go on with us mute objects of our caprice and at last by slightest chance perish ignominiously by the whim of a moment or last on and on—survive us by centuries *equally* by chance! Remember those pitiful relics at Haworth—that half burnt comb of Emily's Milton's snuffbox & mathematical instruments in tortoise shell case. We had an expensive and dull tasting lunch at an old "Coffee House." 400 years old & more. We ate in the Oak Room—old black oak beams etc. Some Oxford students came in. They are dull and unarresting looking young men I regret to say. All the hundreds we saw on the street. We stopped for a moment at the gates of Balliol and thought of Ralph Whitehead. I meant to ~~stay~~ say that at Bod. a very old book with woodcuts of "Oxfordshire Antiquities" was open at a large picture of the old brick Town Hall which stands in middle of our street here at Watlington. Walked about streets & home by way of Abingdon.

UJ Thurs. Oct 31. Washed hair. Wrote letters. Boys dug up qt. of earthworms for chickens & ducks. Letters.

UJ Friday ~~Oct~~ Nov. 1. Partial eclipse of sun viewed at about 11 AM through smoked lamp chimney. Mrs. Newell the help is away for several days went up to London to see the woman for whom her daughter was working as maid in a French chateau when she fell through a skylight and was killed a few weeks ago. I know why English have been such successful colonizers & settlers in heathenish countries. Its because neither aesthetically nor physically are they destroyed by filth. —Such horrors as I have beheld over here. They push it aside put a clean tablecloth on, shine up the brass and eat food fit to throw to the pigs—the drains are a constant menace— cleanliness in the kitchen unknown. Walked briskly late PM toward Ewelme along highway then to left over grown over road we had noted. Soon became a brambly footpath—on until we came to other Ewelme road—then on Icknield Way— home freezing.

Tom Pearce, Tom Pearce, lend me your grey mare
All along, down along, out along lee
For I want to go to Widecombe Fair
With Bill Brewer, Jan Stewer, Peter Gurney, Peter Davy,
Dan'l Whiddon, Harry Hawk, Old Uncle Tom Cobleigh
And all, old Uncle Tom Cobleigh & all.

Using effigies

Old ways of holding up a fellow-villager to scorn by a sort of mob-justice. "Riding to Water" "Mock Burial" "Mock Execution" "Skimmity Riding."

There is a man who lives in this place
Who beats his wife to a sad disgrace

He beats her black & he beats her blue
He beats her till the blood runs through

Now if this man don't mind his manners
We'll have his skin & send to the tanners;
And when the tanners have tanned it well
His hide shall be hung on the nail of hell.

Words supposed to be spoken by people in the country when they look up to the moor on a snowy day "Widecombe folk are plucking their geese—faster faster and faster—" (Widecote old word meaning sky?)

UJ Sat Nov 2. Ironed. Mrs. Newell's father dead and she couldn't do her work here. Late P.M. walked to village meaning to go to old church at Watlington but dark came on very fast & after we had wandered around in the back streets of the village & remarked the secretive, strange atmosphere of the dark little shops (like Chinatown almost)—an inexplicable secret air, we walked home very briskly through a thin misty rain. —Hot chocolate for supper with great blobs of thick cream on top. Boys had great fun with a new lot of plasticine Ellen sent down today—the best they've ever had. — —The most *flexible* — and many beautiful colors (but of course they'll get mixed soon). Garth made an exquisite swan which he left hanging on an invisible thread from a ceiling beam when he went to bed — and a lovely duck—and a falcon. —*Exquisite*—eager poise & balance in flight. Donnan kept us laughing with a very life-like head he made & stuck on the end of a little stick & kept altering the face entirely by a set of disguises (beards, mustaches etc). It looked sometimes like a Sunday-school teacher, at others like one of the murderers in Madam Tussaud's Chamber of Horrors. At others like Arthur Pearce much downtrodden and nervous.

UJ Sunday Nov 3. Mrs. Newell back. —*I* made a grand tapioca pudding & a beefsteak pie. She did a lot of cleaning of all kinds. —In P.M. we went to visit Wayland Smith's Forge, Britwell,

Ewelme, Wallingford, Didcot, Wantage, Vale of Whitehorse, Kingston Lisle, Ashbury, Forge, Ridge Road —etc home.

[**RJ**] If we could have seen the White Horse it would have looked like a foxy wolf, but it is impossible from any road to see more than a leg or two at a time. At Ashbury, when we were there with the Barkans, a red-haired young man told us to drive up the hill to a clump of trees and then walk (or drive if possible) to the next one, but we had not time to go up then. This visit we asked again, to be sure,—another red-haired young man, who sent us up another way. He called the clumps of trees "follies"—the word here for tree-clumps on hill-tops —any conspicuous thing on a height, I suppose. We went up and saw the stones, under one of the three "follies," beyond a wide stubble-field. Una is wary of stubble-fields, since (her) {our}[76] discussion with the farmer here, and asked a young man and woman, who were walking by hay-stacks, how one should go across to the stones. He answered with a grand Irish brogue, astonishing here, "Och," she might just go across, and then back by the Ridge-way. So, after visiting the stones, we drove back toward the great earth-works on White Horse Hill along the Ridge-way—called a Roman road, but I think earlier too. It was completely grassed over, and a foot or two deeper than the adjoining fields, but surprisingly smooth. Wayland's Smithy was a cruciform burial chamber and passage:

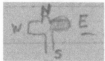

—stones set on edge, the right-hand limb of the cross still covered with its great capstone. Plan very like that of Newgrange. Chambers not more than three feet high from the present ground-level, but very big cap-stones, only one in place, others lying about. Passages oriented with the four quarters, according to Donnan's compass and the red sunset.

---

[76] Una added "our" and the parentheses around "her."

There was a mound, I imagine 100 yds long by 40 broad, not more than four feet high at the highest, which probably once covered the stones also. They stand at the south end of it. Around the outer limits of the mound a low earth-wall and shallow ditch, probably modern, and around these the double row of tall beech trees that make the "folly." No houses or barns in sight, except perhaps far down in the valley. The grassed Ridge-way near by, going toward Uffington "castle" on White Horse hill, and beyond it, "Seven Barrows,"—name of a village or farm, that we noticed on a finger-post. Twilight fell soon, and it was dark when we reached home.

GJ Monday Nov 4 We went to the "Three Pigeons Inn" beyond Tetsworth where there was a hunting meet. The roads were lined with cars, and there were two policemen and one AA man to direct traffic. There was quite a big crowd gathered around watching. The hounds were very eager but ~~very~~ well behaved and were very friendly. There were several women that rode astride but most of them rode side saddle although mother did not think they rode so very well. The horses were very pretty but some were frisky and almost bucked like broncos. At last they started off and went through a gate and up a hill where they stopped while the hounds drew a covert which was empty so they galloped down to the bottom of a valley. We went on aways when a man stopped us and told us not to stop in the bottom of the valley as the fox often went that way so we went on to the other side, where we watched them for a while. After a while we went through a very nice little village and turned down a lane and stopped beside a field into which a lot of the hunt came, presently. In front of them came a harassed looking black pig who did not know which way to go but ran backwards and forwards and finally shot off to the hedge. Two hounds came into the field but were recalled by the horn. Then we went on till the road came to an end. Pretty soon we saw a lot of the horses going along the skyline and disappear in the distance then a whip came back with another man and stood at a gate for a while then the whip galloped off and the other man started back along the road. We went after him in a car till we came to a crossroads where he went one way and we the other. After aways we saw some horses on the skyline. Then we started on a kind of lane to Watlington with two other cars and a motorcycle. We came to a lot of gates which we had to open and close behind us. After about three miles we reached home. The afternoon we stayed in and modeled. [UJ] Mother made a mince pie—

UJ Tues. Nov 5. —Packed. Boys modelled. Exquisite joy to see the leaves floating, swirling, slipping through the air. Autumn in a forest is beautiful.

UJ Wed Nov 6. Up at 7. Started in a rain as usual. To London. Left car at Ladbrook Rd garage to have new hubcap. By tube to Trafalgar Square. Got reservation home Duchess of Bedford Liverpool—New York December 10. —Left in rain from London drove through Guilford to Winchester. *Forests beautiful*—such glorious golden & red colors. The floor of the forests lit up too with the gold. I haven't written enough here of the great happiness we get from autumn colors. It brings back the joy I had in youth in autumn. Today we got out & stood in a small pine forest surrounded by a great beechwood all gold & the dark pines seemed surrounded by flame—a little lake at one side. Dark for last 20 miles hard to drive in the undimmed glare of lamps on motors over here. Such a quaint old inn for the night. Bert Gearing used to tell me about it "Ye old hostel of God-Begot Winchester" (old Tudor house *rebuilt* 1558). Great black oak beams—old black oak carvings low slanting roofs. —Rooms not numbered but named ours is Ethelwulf. Boys is St. Cuthbert. Cedric between. Excellent food. {Saw bedroom at Godbegot where Queen of Roumania slept. Enormous oak beam over bed. —Dates from 1062. Empress Matilda room.}

RJ [Thursday] {Nov. 7}[77] In the morning wandered through
cavernous little lanes (the boys called them wyrds,
remembering their Scotland) and visited the Great Hall—
speaking-tube in masonry above remains of Norman dais,
through which the king could call his guards at need—Arthur's
round-table on wall—foundations of Charles II's unfinished
palace (Winchester barracks)— custodian an enthusiast about
stones—Caen, Purbeck, Portland—even flint, of which he
brought us a lump to show, and told of a huge piece that a
farmer plowed up, he tried to buy it but the farmer would not
sell.— Winchester Cathedral—stone portraits of naked
bishops a few months post-mortem—must tempt young
medical students—bones of William Rufus, Canute, etc.
suspended half way to the ceiling in painted wooden chests.
[UJ] Lucky to hear superb pipe organ here. **[RJ]** Drove to
Amesbury. The many barrows. Stonehenge so much more
imposing than we had hoped. Curious gray vertical bands on
each lintel-stone, entirely symmetrical,

two on each face of each stone. Apparently smooth stripes
bare of lichen. Similar stripes on the uprights, but these at
random and of all sizes, across and along. I can't imagine what
chance of wind or water could make the stripes on the lintels:
but how could they be artificial? Intrusive vivid thought of
Tess[78] and Angel Clare running into these stones during their
terrified hopeless flight in the darkness. A Royal Air Force
plane hovering above the stones, darting low above them like
a big wasp. My left upper wisdom tooth collapsed at this place
and I gave it for an offering. **[UJ]** Bitter cold wind blowing.
Wide plain spread out. Mist & drizzle at times. My mind

---

[77] Added by Una.
[78] Tess Durbeyfield, the heroine of *Tess of the d'Urbervilles*, a novel by Thomas
Hardy. Here, Robinson refers to Tess and her husband Angel Clare's flight
to Stonehenge after Tess has murdered her seducer.

refuses—isnt able to relate these people of Stonehenge time to *us*. Felt like snow. —Boys adored games about the stones.

Petition to Pope Honorius III in 1217 to allow removal of Cathedral from Old Sarum. Complaint states

"They state that the Cathedral Church, being within the line of defense (of Castle) is subject to so many inconveniences that the Canons cannot live there without danger to life.

"Being in a raised place the continued gusts of wind make such a noise that the clerks can hardly hear one another sing & the place is so rheumatic by reason of the wind that they often suffer in health.

"The Church they say is so shaken by wind & storm, that it daily needs repair & the site is without trees & grass & being of chalk has such a glare that many of the clerks have lost their sight.

"Water they say is only to be got from a distance & often at a price that elsewhere would buy enough for a whole district.

"If the clerks have occasion to go in & out on business they cannot do so without leave of the Castellan: so that on Ash Wednesday, Holy Thursday & on Synodal & ordination & other solemn days the faithful who wish to visit the Church cannot do so the keepers of the Castle declaring that the defenses would be endangered.

"Moreover as many of the clerks have no dwellings there they have to hire them from the soldiers, so that few are found able & willing to reside on the spot."

So in 1220 the foundation for Cathedral was laid at Salisbury not far away & in 1227 Old Sarum church was abandoned. Some of the tombs & bodies & memorials & slabs were removed to Salisbury. We looked through the window of a closed hut inside Castle fortification & saw carved remnants of the Cathedral building, they have fine, elaborately & finely carved stone figures mostly very grotesque. [RJ] On to Old Sarum, where we walked about in a drizzle of rain among the stumps of flint-and-stone walls. Incredible quantities of flints, here as in Oxfordshire. The circumvallation—very high and steep earthworks. [UJ] cf great columns more gigantic than anywhere else of granite with other small columns. Purbeck marble. [RJ] Down to Salisbury, and visited the cathedral.

> "We are half sick of cathedrals," said
> Garth and Donnan and Robin.

We drove to Blandford and stopped at the "Gown." Steam-heated! And the weather turned warmer too, so that we were comfortable in the evening, and oppressed at night, though windows wide open. Stoop-shouldered old waiter, dutiful and reverend.

RJ [Friday] {Nov. 8.}[79] We stopped and drove about in Bere Regis for Hardy's sake, and at Wool eyed Woolbridge manor, with the poultry about it, but for lack of direction did not look up the abbey-ruins where the stone coffin is. Drove around by East Lulworth, where the tank and armored car hangars of modern war compete with the great earthworks of prehistoric wars that cup the hill-tops. Then down to the shingle of Lulworth Cove,—the boys their most favorite amusement, chucking stones into water—and so around into Dorchester. First we went and revered Max Gate, hidden in its trees, peering out at a high column miles away on the moor that I suppose is the monument to Nelson's Hardy.[80] Then into the town—statue to William Barnes—out the Bridport road, past great earthworks that were no doubt Maiden Castle and the other one. We had asked a deaf half-witted wagon-driver the way to the Maumbury Rings—he thought toward Bridport. We turned about and came back and visited the Rings—queer and quite impressive. A greyhound taking its exercise saluted the boys. Then we visited Stinsford church—beautiful, quiet, hidden away—first, misdirected by a friendly old man, we went back to Max Gate, and had to come around from there.

---

[79] Added by Una.
[80] Vice-Admiral Thomas Masterman Hardy.

(On the head of the stone slab.)
Here lies the heart of Thomas Hardy, O.M.,
Son of Thomas and Jemima Hardy.
He was born at Upper Bockhampton, 2 June 1840, and died at Max Gate, Dorchester, 11 January 1928. His ashes rest in Poets' Corner, Westminster Abbey.
(On the side of the stone)
Here is buried Emma Lavinia, wife of Thomas Hardy, O.M., and daughter of John Attersoll — (Name has rubbed in my pocket from the paper it was scribbled on.)[81]
She was born at Plymouth, Nov. 24, 1840, lived at St. Juliot, Cornwall, 1868–1873, and died at Max Gate, Dorchester, August 27, 1912.
This for remembrance.

[UJ] At Stinsford church—the grotesque gargoyles—one holding his mouth (spout) open with both hands, such a *beautiful* church.
[RJ] Little stone-circle, two big and a number of small stones, found off in the corner of an estate on the Dorchester to Bridport road.
Through Bridport, etc., headlong descent into Lyme Regis, which we had given as our address on our wedding announcements in 1913, and never seen till now. The "Three Cups" was closed, the Red Lion looked dark, we went up a very steep pavement to the Alexandra.
People in evening dress, two of them the owners of Langmoor Manor, flushed with the success of the auction which that day had sold off their furniture. Perhaps the other man in evening dress had bought the estate, it appeared so from the conversation. We had passed Langmoor while the auction was proceeding, and marvelled at the many motors.
[UJ] At Exeter Cathedral brilliant sunlight pouring through stained glass along one whole side—incredibly beautiful & the

---

[81] "Gifford" was the name rubbed away.

cathedral alight & aflame with it. Finely carved font of
cathedral hundreds of figures.

RJ [Saturday] {Nov. 9.}[82] We walked about Lyme Regis and left
about eleven **[UJ]** & thought about our "At Home at Lyme
Regis" on our marriage announcements. **[RJ]** Astonished at the
littleness of Axminster. Visited Exeter Cathedral, drove on into
Dartmoor. We walked about and saw many hut-circles—
(stone-circles—*big* stones)—without going to Grimspound.
Dartmoor granite in its crystals, structure, color,
decomposition, so wonderfully like our own at Tor House.
Grim Princetown. The great "clapper bridge" at Postbridge. A
slab of granite that seemed to me 15 or 16 feet long by 7½
wide, then two narrower slabs side by side, then a third like the
first, on piers of well-made dry-stone masonry of big squared
stones. Stairs at each end, but broken down at one end. The
slenderer long slabs of the middle span look like ~~modern~~ more
recent repair-work. I love big ancient stones.
Launceston was crowded with people for a concert and the
armistice day celebrations. The carved stone-doorway through
which we entered the "White Hart" is 800 years old, taken
from the ruins of the priory there. The hallway was stuffed with
an extraordinary boss of innumerable chrysanthemums. The
boys devoured a new book of Sherlock Holmes stories—their
birthday, poor blessings—while we wandered about the streets
in the dark buying luncheon materials for the morrow, and
gazing at the marvelously carved granite walls of the little
church. **[UJ]** White Hart old coaching inn, —& as we came
into old stables stone paved now used as garage (enormous
around courtyard) about 20 high traps were being harnessed to
horses & country squires some with their ladies were waiting
to set out. Lanterns to & fro. {Found here an edition
(monumental) of Baring Gould's "English Minstrelsy" copied
out old song "Blow, blow thou winter wind." Shakespeare}

---

[82] Added by Una.

In his haste Robin didn't say half enough about Dartmoor—its utter wildness—wide windswept spaces, tors in every direction. Dried gorse & heather, high shrill wild whinnying of untamed moor ponies, boys chased them. They got out into the cold blast while we were eating lunch & soon located stone circles & remains of the old stone hut dwellings. They took us to them there high on the hill & we spanked each boy 13 + 1 times, it being their 13th birthday. Spanked in a stone circle. Ages since a child had been spanked there. Going down out of Dartmoor we saw standing all alone an old misshapen cross leaning over drunkenly. We took a picture. We saw the fingerpost to *Widdicombe* {Widecombe}. (Have just finished reading Phillpott's "Fair.") Amazing how *wet* the high moor is. Water doesn't run off it. Air very invigorating. How lonely this moor must be with snow on it. Shuddered at grim gray walls of Dartmoor prison in distance. Thought of miserable wretches there. These moors are dangerous for strangers because of the bogs.

Nov 6
  Britwell Salome
  Watlington
  Stokenchurch
  Wycombe
  Beaconsfield
  Uxbridge
  London
  Richmond
  Kingston
  Esher
  Guildford
  Winchester[X]
  Stockbridge
  Amesbury
Nov 7
  Stonehenge

Old Sarum
Salisbury
Blandford[X]
Bere Regis
Nov 8
  Wool
  Dorchester
  Winterbourne Abbas
  Bridport
  Lyme Regis[X]
  Axminster
  Honiton
Nov 9
  Exeter[X]
  Moretonhampstead
  Princetown
  Two Bridges

Dartmoor
Tavistock
Milton Abbot
Launceston^X
Five Lanes Inn
Bolventor

Nov 10
Jamaica Inn
Dozmare Pool
St Neot
Lostwithiel
Grampound
Probus
Truro
Helston
Lizard
Helston
Marazion

Nov 11
Penzance
Newlyn
Mousehole
Lands End
Sennen
St Just
Pendeen
Mowah
Zennor
St Ives^X

Nov 12
St Ives
Zennor
St Ives
Uny Lelant
Hayle
Camborne
Redruth
Zelah

Mitchell
St Columb Major
Wadebridge
Camelford
Delabole Quarries
Tintagel^X

Nov 13
Tintagel
Boscastle
Bude
Kilkhampton
Morwenstow
Bideford

Nov 14
Bideford
Barnstaple
S. Molton
Bampton
Taunton
Glastonbury
Wells
Cathedrals
Winchester
Salisbury
Exeter
Truro
Glastonbury
Wells

Nov 15 Wells
Frome
Trowbridge
Devizes
Avebury
Swindon
Asbury
Wantage
Wallingford
Britwell Salome

UJ [Sunday] Nov. 10. Out of Launceston after another look at the church. Went inside—tiny, tiny stone stairs in thickness of wall. Rain & lots of hail. Turned from main road at Jamaica Inn by a lane rough & wet for a mile or so by cart track across wild moor to Dozmare (pronounce Dozmary) Pool where Excalibur was thrown—not as weird and strange and dark as I had pictured it—though lovely enough—all by itself in the moor (2 tiny stone huts not far away but they melted into the stone walls & stone piles). Got out & stood on stone wall to avoid bog in bitter wind to look and think about it. Tors & rocky hills all about. —On miles through muddy stoney narrow lane came to stone house asked if we could go on that way through St Neot [RJ] and the girl said "yes," but that was not the last time we stopped to ask of old men and young, women and boys. We fell into a wrinkle of the mountain and were in St. Neot, a grain of a village, with ancient church. The few inhabitants were just leaving church and looked severely at us. St. Neot was a hunch-backed dwarf, and a brother of King Alfred. When he died his body was taken to St. Neots in Huntingdonshire, but later brought back to this Cornish village. Finally his bones were scattered all over the moor by a revel of drunkards and so lost. We were now in search of Lostwithiel. We climbed a great hill from St. Neot and fell down so steep and gravelly a one that I got out and ran behind to lighten the car. Asked directions at a lodge, the lodge-keeper knew little but a gray-eyed woman from the manor, who was there with a dog, set us in train again.

[UJ] {At Marazion, (Godolphin Hotel) see next page. Mr. McClelland was talking about pronunciation of English names. Cirencester called *Sirister* by many people. The natives pronounce it Siren.

Fine spire at Salisbury highest in England. At Truro new cathedral shut in & spoiled by crowding buildings. Heard here marvellous chimes—finer than I've ever heard before.

In our village at Britwell is a sign "— —Carpenter & Undertaker." We saw a sign in Cornwall at Phillack "Builder, Contractor & Undertaker."

—In morning at Marazion tempest still raging. We looked down—at our feet several wagons 2 horses each hitched tandem—loaded with seaweed. —Several men busily pitch-forking it on. —Used for fertilizer. Always plentiful after storm & high waves. Very picturesque in the storm. Just before we reached Launceston passed an exquisite old manor house at Milton Abbot. Long low of stone with a little bell tower at one end & coach drive through arch passage in house to courtyard.} **[RJ]** Truro was all in the street preparing for an armistice parade, and the chimes jetted from the high new cathedral. **[UJ]** Yellow gorse on Cornish moors. **[RJ]** The Lizard, we left the car to walk on the cliff, and at once the wind was full of rain. High sliding cliffs, filmy tamarisks enduring the wind, huge funnel-shaped hole through the top of the cliff below the lighthouse, to where a cave had fallen in, called the Lion's Den. The lighthouse lenses began to revolve while we watched them, and soon to shine. Wind blew, sunset reddened, we drove back to Helston, and west, intending for Penzance, but suddenly around a turn in the rainy darkness we saw St Michael's Mount like a giant in the sea with a light or two shining toward its summit.

"Where the great angel of the guarded mount
    Looks toward Namancos and Bayona's hold—"[83]

A hotel appeared by the road immediately, and we were so fascinated that we stopped, there in Marazion. Only asking rooms looking toward the sea and the Mount.

"Look homeward, angel, now, and melt with ruth,
    And O ye dolphins — "

---

[83] From Milton's "Lycidas." Robinson has substituted "angel" for "vision." He continues the quote four lines on.

The *Godolphin* Hotel. Furious wind, rain and hail all night. Affable and admirable Anglo-Irishman the only other guest. Born in County Down, civil service in Malaysia, sixty years old or so. Unattached and tired of the Riviera, taken Grebe House, near Marazion, but house not in repair yet. In North Ireland once, returning there, he saw his father's name over a pub— Robert McClelland. He went in, and the man who sold him a drink was the image of his father. He said to the man "How do you account for it?" "Och, simple it is. Your grandfather had many brothers, and they didn't always do right." —I said "And Ireland has such a reputation for chastity." "But not," he said, "Northern Ireland." [UJ] {McClelland a friend of Baring-Gould's[84] son. Often stayed with them. Heard him talk much of Hawker.[85]}

UJ [Monday] Nov. 11. It was visitors' day at the Castle & boys & I at least would have loved to go over but the raging sea covered the causeway or breakwater path & torrents of rain fell. So we had to forego it. [RJ] The storm was so furious that we didn't leave until noon. In Penzance Una bought a lot of little Cornish crosses, of grayish soft stone like the one she loves, and other cut-stones, for gifts. [UJ] Gray stone = polyphant. Each cross is cut like some real one of the district. We have seen so many of them in unexpected places, in a hedge or at a crossroad or in a yard or in a cemetery—or standing alone in a field worn, misshapen yet dignified and *each* a personality. They are not firm and cold or *trim*—each has some *quirk*—a bit of mischief or drollery somehow—and loveable and how thoroughly a part of the region. Boys & I bought several tiny compasses, round, of serpentine & 2 jars of lovely green blue serpentine & 2 tiny crystal balls & some

---

[84] The Reverend Sabine Baring-Gould, Anglican clergyman, novelist, and antiquarian.
[85] The Reverend Robert Stephen Hawker, Anglican clergyman, poet, and antiquarian of Cornwall.

lovely amber. The prices at this shop (Cornish Stone Co Promenade Penzance) are extremely reasonable & I felt I had made some wonderful purchases. Then we drove through blinding rain through picturesque Newlyn and Mousehole (pronounce Muzzle) up & down steep hills along the coast. Saw several more crosses by the way. On by poor road through wild country the car often tottering with the impact of wind to Lands End. Wild and rocky, foam dashing high, slender little ghost of Longships lighthouse just showing through the swirling rain & waves. Ate our lunch in lee of hotel sitting tight in car. I went into hotel, (nearly blown over), to buy postcards & saw three more crosses but they were too smoothly cut almost like machine cutting & 2/ more each than at Penzance. Robin braved the tempest to snatch a stone from Lands End rocks. Boys & I gazed at landscape. On again by better road, we found we had not been on the main road before, to St Just & then to Zennor where we had been expecting to rent a house (through the kind efforts of Virginia Woolf) before we decided to sail Dec. 10. —We had asked to have our mail forwarded there and found letters from Bender & Lehman[86] etc. A wild desolate little muddy village set in a depression of the hills with great stones in every direction. *The Tinner's Arms* (where our brass warming-pan came from!). We expected to stay here several days but the man (looked like a sailor) who came reluctantly to door when I kept knocking said he couldn't take us. He had beds but never kept more food than his family needed in winter. Scene dominated by church. —Gray, gray, gray everywhere. In churchyard 2 misshapen short crosses have been set up over tombs (slab) of two brothers who lie side by side name Borlase one an admiral, other Vicar of this parish. I suppose the Vicar was an enthusiast, had perhaps rescued them from a pigsty or stepping stone. Friendly helpful postmistress said she could have put us up if she had known

---

[86] Benjamin Lehman, professor of English at the University of California, Berkeley.

in time to manage. —On through rain up steep hills—eternal granite rocks & hills 4 miles to St. Ives. Down the crowded little streets, steep & twisty. —Then up to a very fine hotel *Chy-an-Albany*. Really first class, fine dinner & big fires & enormous cat. Boys have 2 (complete) volumes of Sherlock Holmes which occupy them every moment when they are not travelling. I wrote letters. The people down here act much more vigorous & alive than down in the Midlands. Little stone churches down here often have quaint or finely carved little stone shutters (carved holes for ventilation) near top of tower.

UJ Tuesday Nov 12. Brilliant sunshine & sharp cold wind with high scudding white clouds & occasional showers. We walked about the village & bought food & a pot of Cornish cream. Decided to drive back & gaze at Zennor by sunlight. A fine wide view over sea. High hills, ships, —Zennor as wild as ever by sunlight. It was *this* morning visit we saw the crosses in the churchyard. Couldn't find out whereabouts of either Zennor cromlech or Lagan stone. Postmistress said a very large stone was on hill on way to St. Ives by a quarry. When we got there Robin & Garth went up to see it. They stayed a long time looking about. Wide wide view over hills & sea, sharp biting wind, tumult & chaos of rocks—on a granite rock was newly cut carefully but not professionally "W. H. Hudson often came here." They could also see a tarn like Dozmare Pool inland in a depression of hills. No birds or cattle. No houses even except the little hamlet of Zennor with its gray church guarding it. Sheep dung ~~amongst~~ in long grass among rocks. —Back to St. Ives. I got out & wrote a card to Tom Bickle from his birthplace as I had promised. Then to Uny Lelant where is a little old church with sand dunes held down by long planted rushy grass. Here was once a village covered now & lost under sand, 'tis said but the place was not as wild & beautiful as I had expected. —A neat village too near & a golf course. On then until we came to St Columb Major. We had heard that the little Cornish cross I bought so long ago at Tintagel was copied from one here & Robin got out in the cold gray light at 3:30 (seemed about to snow) found it *is* my cross. Almost overwhelmed by a curious slate slab next to it with a queer error on it. Says in purport

> John— so & so died aged 15 months.
> Their daughters died —date & age (That's all on it)

I took boys' picture by St Columb Major's cross. On to Camelford (Camelot of King Arthur). Looked for Slaughter Bridge but although we were close to it we didn't find it in the twilight (where Arthur was supposed to have been fatally wounded). —On through the incredible piles of slate (gleaming in rain) of Delabole Quarries to Tintagel which I thought the most romantic place I saw over here before. I stayed at the King Arthur's Castle Hotel on the cliffs before when with Bert Gearing. Now we stopped at the Wharncliffe Arms an old hotel almost opposite the XIV century stone house in village. Two young women in charge. We were only guests but a very excellent dinner was provided in a little red sitting room with a hot fire of sea coals in fireplace. Robin bought us a bottle of Scotch whisky. Very pleasant evening. — Boys reading & we writing etc. Two compatriots from Maine (dowdy but with grand car & chauffeur) came in late & unexpected & shared our room for half hour before going to bed. It was bitter cold. We have been through rain & hail & sleet this trip.

UJ Wed. Nov. 13. After good breakfast, we started to walk to Castle (about ¾ mile from village). Stopped by a mite of an old crone with 2 fangs & an elfish look & a commanding tone who said she had the key to castle door but was on her way to buy a bit of meat & would attend to us later. We said we would go to the church first. She conducted me at my request into the shop where I got my little cross so many years ago. The old lady had only commonplace polished serpentine ones. She said her husband had died & no one else could make them. She said that she could sell hundreds if she had them. A woman in London for whom her husband made a big cross, was bringing it back to place in little church a mile or so away now being restored "and I can go & see it, mum," with a quaver. {In yard of Wharncliffe Arms are 2 old crosses one just a fragment from the village. One is mentioned in the Doomsday Book.} —Out again into biting bracing cold. —Along a high path to St Materiana church. It used to be said that here the gravestones had to be anchored down so great is the wind blowing always. {Finest most precipitous cliff scenery in Cornwall. Lundy dim in distance.} Inside the gate to right is a rude cross made of ship timber. On it hangs an old life buoy cut from a ship wrecked near here & under them lies an Italian sailor drowned in that wreck. Inside church many interesting things—one a Roman mile stone, & a very ancient brass set into pavement & a Norman font (in an alcove under a carpet). A young man, curate I think, who was filling lamps found it for us. —He also took us into the little Lady Chapel where lamp was burning. — On along cliff path to Castle. Bright sun but so damp & cold we would have just viewed it from the cliff if we had not known the little old witch was waiting in hut with key. —We got it & up a steep path cut into rock through locked door. (No one is allowed to go in wind & rain storm it's too slippery). —All very quiet and beautiful on this high hill cliff—when I was here before a few sheep grazed. It is steeped in story this place.

{Tintagel Castle "The residew of the buildings of the Castel be sore weatherbeaten and yn ruins: but it hath been a large thinge." Leland[87] (1540).}

—After a good look about we went down. —Boys and Robin went below to cave filled with green light & foam of sea through the cave open at both ends. {Small flat round stones near cave. People here collected them and have them around

---

[87] John Leland, English poet and antiquary.

doorstops here. We took one for Tor House.} I went back to hut bought cards. She made us sign visitors book. Showed "the young gentlemen" signatures of Royalty—also the name of a lady from Turkey ("from all corners of the globe you see my young gentlemen"). She was feeding an old sea gull when we came. She'd had it since before the war. Noon now, still very cold. We had to get away quietly from hotel (after changing shoes) because a sick man (motorist) had stopped there & a doctor was being sought. Nervous fur-coated wife pacing garden. In courtyard of this inn is the biggest stone trough we have seen big and deep.

Down through edge of Boscastle without noticing it, being troubled about a noise in engine. —At Bude we noticed our indicator (showing recharging) was stationary. Stopped at good garage at Bude. They found a broken wire in magneto & repaired it. There 1½ hrs. We walked down to Bude Breakwater paved with huge stones. A marvelous place high tide & wind icy cold. Boys skipped stones faces red as cherries. {We do not see hedges covered with berries down here as in Oxfordshire but *stone* walls.}

On to Morwenstow although so near twilight I had to see Stephen Hawker's place. A beautiful little church with zig-zag carving over arched doorway. A girl was playing pipe organ inside in dusk with one candle her old mother pumping handle. Saw in churchyard the white painted figure-head (a Highland warrior with claymore & kilt & shield) of a ship {the brig *Caledonia* wrecked 1842} marking grave of 20 or so drowned sailors. We looked down into the ravine & on a level space was the mansion Hawker built with its curious chimneys (like different church towers & the kitchen one like his mother's tomb). It looks quite empty and desolate. We could see over the door a plate set in, on it is carved we know the stanza by him beginning

> "A house, a glebe, a pound a day
> A pleasant place to watch & pray

Be true to church, be kind to poor
O minister, forevermore."

{2 old stone stiles & lych-gate in wall. An old Cornish cross just inside gate.} We drove away in twilight thinking of Hawker. Snow & hail on road. Passed turning to Clovelly but it was cold & dark & slippery with light snow. I didn't feel like the bother of that steep street of steps in Clovelly and having to walk to hotel with luggage. On to Bideford where we fared well. Had a fire in our bedroom but were martyrs to it because the grate was rickety & we couldn't leave it for fear it would fall out into room coals & all. Fires for evening cost 1/ or 1/6 or 2/. Only Americans order them apparently.

Woke up & gazed upon that "old Esquire of a bridge." Talked about men of Devon & drove away in the rain. Awful din of chimes in evening because of mayor's dinner. Went on & on! Snow still standing on thatched roofs.

UJ Thurs. Nov 14. This day nervous because of engine noise. Stopped at 2 garages & had inspected—no result. 1st thought it universal joint or transmission, 2nd thought dragging brakes. —We didn't dare go over rough road of Exmoor through Doone Valley as we had planned. Disappointed. Looked into cathedral at Glastonbury. Thought of Joseph of Arimathea. Saw the stone coffin he was buried in, here. {Glastonbury = Avalon in fable.} On to Wells saw Cathedral dim & beautiful. No hotel recommended in RAC book here, but we found a very good one (and old) The Swan opposite Cathedral. Some grand (& friendly) Americans from Boston. Fire in room— trouble about hot water bottles. I had left my two at Blandford & not recovered them yet. Boys went to bed & Robin read aloud Sherlock Holmes. I *sat* & combed hair! {In several of the Cathedrals we have seen beautiful alabaster effigies. They grow a beautiful color and texture with age.}

UJ Friday Nov 15. Went out & bought a silver swan salt holder like those old ones used in hotel. Bought some stale bread & cakes to feed swans on moat filled by springs of Episcopal palace. Went there by private gate of Swan Hotel. Swans & ducks ("Oswald Jinkinses" say boys). They had a jolly time feeding them. Very lovely & the brilliant yellow leaves drifting down gently & the bitter pleasant smell of dried leaves in the air. —To Cathedral. Space in here magnificent. Heard beautiful singing as a service was going on in one chapel when we first came. Boys of course much amused. We watched the clock strike 11. Made by monk of Glastonbury (1325). A man-size figure above & at the right kicks and hits a gong. Around the top of clock knights in armor on horseback joust & one is killed & falls backward. Remember here XIV cent golden window exquisite glass. The underground crypt with stone coffins, etc. Most of all the *beautiful* stone steps leading to Chapter House. Midway up they go in 2 directions —one to Chapter House, & other up over gate. From the general shape & contour of the steps aided by the worn down places in stone surface they look like flowing water. **[RJ]** In Wells Cathedral, in memory of Humfredus Willis, armiger; Latin on a bronze plate on the wall; translated into English by Chief Justice Lord Coleridge:

> "My worse part lives, my better buried lies;
> Death is my life; that he may live he dies;
> To earth I trust these ashes, and my woe;
> 'Till to this dust, I too as dust may go;
> 'Tis thus disconsolate a widow sings.
> T.P. her cousin hopes for better things."

Also in Wells, inscription in honor of Bishop Still, who, among other noble acts, endowed "an almshouse for six poor old decayed and impotent burgesses of Wells." Why is Una so delighted with the *words*? "Poor, old, decayed and impotent . . ." **[UJ]** The inscription is on a brass plate covered with illustrations & phrases in Latin. The lady kneels & prays, there

is a large broken tree with leaves on it. (Says "Broken not dead"). Then a square with things the knight had left behind him, plumed hat, sword, gloves with gauntlets, high boots, lute, etc. Another monument shows a figure of a young girl looking at 2 urns containing ashes of her parents (canon & wife killed in bed by fall of chimneys in close). Very cold as we went through Somerset & along edge of Salisbury plain. Saw sheets of ice on ponds. Ducks walking about on ice. Many sheep in this district. Beautiful they are in the lovely wattled fences they use down here. (Woven rushes or reeds). The fences are in small sections & easily moveable. Gray sky (like snow) gray hills, gray plains, gray fences, gray sheep—all shading into gray except the great flock of intensely black rooks I scared up when I took a picture of the sheep. —On to Avebury. The largest stones in England in stone circle. Little ancient village inside stone circle. The stones are many times larger than Stonehenge but unhewn and shapeless. We see tumuli in every direction on the plain. [RJ] Silbury Hill—I ignorantly assured the boys that it was much too big to be artificial. Enormous earth-work and ditch around the stones, reaching far beyond the limits of the village—what a labor for wooden shovels carved with flint knives! Earth-works last longer than stone works. The stones are said to be sarsen sand-stone, but they don't look like the ones at Stonehenge, but like limestone. [UJ] On in cold, bought provisions on way & got to Kerry Vor at 6:00 in rain. We were glad to be in our own place again & Robin soon had bright fires roaring & I the steak cooked & boys sat down quickly to model with their beloved plasticine.
Sometime a few miles after leaving Avebury saw an excellent energetic horse cut in the chalk hill. *Much* better than one near Kingston Lisle. There is said to be another near here. We did not see it.

UJ Sat. Nov 16. Rain! Boys happily modelled. I went to village in rain for supplies. Awfully wet tragic little man followed me into cream shop said "Um look like a drowned rat, don't I, mum?"

Said he was from Cornwall—said he was fed up with life—
started to tramp. Slept out all last night in awful wet & cold.
Said he was son of sailor—gave him a copper for a bit of
lavender. At bedtime it was freezing. We sat up until 1:45 A.M.
reading & writing.

"Thou art thy mother's glasse, and she in thee
Calls back the lovely April of her prime." Shakespeare[88]

[RJ] The houses have flint walls, brick coigns, and vertical ribs
of brick dividing the flint into panels; except some that are
brick with half-timbering, and a few wholly brick. The walls are
usually only a foot thick, or even eight inches. Often they have
settled outward and are propped up with buttresses. Roofs
mostly of small flat tiles, gray-red lichened. [UJ] Garden walls
same construction.

UJ Sunday Nov 17. {Thermometer didn't get up to 40° at any time
today. About 38° at noon. Evening 32°} Fair cold bright
sunshine. Boys played out, let ducks onto pond. There is an
owl living in this garden and at night it hoots and calls at

---

[88] Sonnet 3, lines 9–10.
[89] St. Nicholas Church.

intervals. We went out for a brisk walk in late P.M. Boys hilarious with the brisk air. We went down a lane to get a look at the little church. Its hidden away near a few old barns with a huge house (perhaps the vicarage) behind. —Robin read aloud the Irish novel The Big House at Inver by Œ Somerville. Garth is always much interested in the moveable poultry houses we see on the big farms here. Coops on a cart which can be drawn from field to field and left for a few days until the stubble is gleaned of grain. Throughout England we have observed the yew trees. There seem to be about an equal number of English & Irish yews. English are of more spreading habit, limbs flexible and plumy & drop downward, Irish (like our little ones at Tor House) are of close growing habit, limbs tend upward. Foliage has a slightly silverish or gray tint, lighter than the dark hue of English yews. We like the Irish better but both are very beautiful. In the close near the moat of Bishops palace at Wells we saw the most beautiful & perfectly symmetrical specimen of English yew tree yet. {Sunday evenings about 6:30 we hear lovely ringing of bells. Churches at Britwell Salome, Watlington & Ewelme. One has a sweet chime.}

UJ Mon. Nov 18 Tiresome day. Went to Oxford to find out the rubbing noise in car. —Cold & a dense fog could see but a few yards ahead of car. Hard to drive. They messed about haphazardly all day until 3:15 before they had an idea of trouble. We left the car there finally. They thought it was a dry bearing or broken one in rear axle. We had good lunch (fish & chips) & then shopped & sat in station for a while (until a little boy came in, all swathed up, mumps or something) so we got out. {Bought newspapers, and a poultry magazine for Garth & an H. G. Wells book for Donnan.} Sat in library for a while. Came home by 4:00 bus. Too bitter cold & freezing all day to sightsee. Walked from Watlington. Very cold. —Soon after we came home it grew warmer (40°) & began to rain & blow violently. I made *delicious* biscuits for supper. Today in Oxford

Donnan said "I know what makes this fog—Its the steam coming out of all these peoples mouths." Oxford a dreary place. Boring looking people with red noses. Robin said tonight "Think of a climate where the breath comes out in a steaming vapor all day like a running horse." —He had been brushing his teeth in the cold kitchen.

A significant thing. In U.S. there are dozens of magazines of war stories, battle stories etc. Here not one is found. (Poor Donnan!)

Always meant to write down this, à propos Irish love of fighting. A man coming back to his native village after years' absence sees a disturbance in street & asks eagerly "And is it a private quarrel it is, or can anyone join in?"

[RJ] {On our return from Cornwall, I think between Devizes and Avebury, we passed through a haunted place called Borough Bridge. A good-sized stone church looked very little on the top of a great artificial mound. There was more feeling of antiquity than at Avebury even. We paid tuppence to cross a toll-bridge. I said "It's the most haunted place we've seen." Later I saw a picture of standing stone there, which we didn't see.}

[UJ] Next writing I shall describe Kerry Vor.

UJ Tues Nov 19. Dreary day. Garth got up with a badly swollen finger middle of left hand. No reason we could see unless poison from a furze bush he fell into a week ago at Tintagel. He got a dozen or more tiny thorns in—one in this knuckle he didn't get out—

Rain & wind all day & cold. Called up Doctor King Edwards Biddys doctor at Watlington. Said his office hours are 6 PM— 9 PM! Car didn't get done. Coxeter[90] phoned. I made Garth soak his finger in hot water for 3 hrs. Started out in wild wind & mist hours it seemed after dark to Dr. and to market. We had to walk way beyond Watlington toward station. Doctor

---

[90] The mechanic working on the Jefferses' car.

attended by abrupt but expert nurse. Couldn't see any reason for swelling. Said to keep hot fomentation on for several days & keep arm in sling. Not much pain but hurts if you press near knuckle. Dr scraped a hole in the place where thorn had been. Walked home against stiff wind. I felt strangely tired. {Shampoos for Robin, Garth & Donnan.}

UJ Wed ~~Thu~~ Nov 20. Donnan got sick in night vomiting, diarrhea etc. I too felt sick & tummy-ache. We think it grapes which we ate at supper. Robin as usual thinks the milk is infected. Donnan stayed in bed all day. Garth & I put hot fomentations on his finger. Swelling & soreness subsiding slowly. Tonight we all sat by fire in Donnan's room & read. Garth suddenly vomited so he's got it too. Donnan is feeling better. Broth for his supper. Garth let the ducks out onto the pond today for a while. Sunshine warm 52°. Robin walked to village this morning accompanied by Kooch and did the shopping. A telephone message from Coxeter says Ford in order again. I'll go get it in morning.

Kerry Vor is an old house. History known for over 200 yrs.

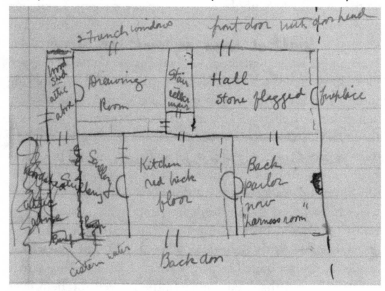

Kitchen should have been drawn larger. I had woodshed
drawn in wrong place at first.

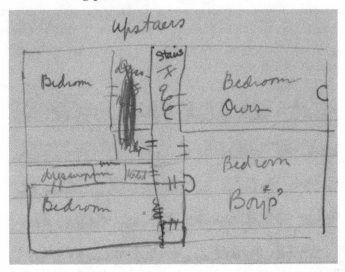

{In 2 rooms or 3 wide 12 or 14 in old floor boards of dark
oak. There is a cellar underneath}
It is stone plastered over. Inside I haven't attempted to indicate
all the cupboards & nooks & closets in every room. In kitchen
above one door leads up a back stair, now cut off by toilet. The
kitchen is the pleasantest room in house. Very large fireplace
& copper & brass utensils about. Gay Breton china on dresser.
Floor bright red brick. Walls & wood-panelling white. Drawing
room French windows open into walled garden with a white
bench & rose trellis. —The garden is very large many yew trees.
In the back garden are stables & chicken houses & sheds for
traps & cars & out buildings of all kinds, one an old brick was
extra rooms for house formerly with 2 fireplaces brick floor &
tiny diamond leaded glass windows—old dim glass. An old
well with windlass (—our drinking water) trellis around it. The
wall is partly red brick, partly flint. The red brick in tiers at
intervals & along top & bottom. There is a garden gate in wall
in the direction pointed by arrow which leads to a lane across
which is an old thatched cottage. Mrs. Newell the help lives

there. A duck pond lies outside wall beyond drawing room. It is marked X.[91] There is a kitchen garden, cabbage, onions etc & a number of old apple & pear trees. Opposite the duck pond across the narrow road another old house is the P.O. & in it lives Mrs. Rivett who does the laundry & comes in 1 day a week to clean or do any extra work at odd hours. Her brother cobbles our shoes. She has twins! There are 5 cats. Amy, Puck, Mrs. Catt, Sylvester, Bogie. Boys are cross because I don't let them stay in the house & sit on the table! Kooch is Newell's dog. He is a "Shepherd's Bush Terrier"! (i.e. fox terrier & anything at all, found in the pound at Shepherd's Bush). He has a waggish deprecatory look as he watches me carefully to see how many privileges he will get. {43° at midnight.}

UJ Thurs. Nov 21. —Warmer 52° sunny. Got up at 7:30 no breakfast. Left house at 8 to walk to Watlington to catch the Oxford bus to go for car. I waited by the Anchor & Bull Inn for one hour! It was due actually at 9:07 instead of 8:45 as we had thought & besides had broken down. Got our car & provisions & home by noon. Heavenly to have car again. Donnan better & Garth's finger better. Things picking up. Rode to Watlington in P.M. In evening fire in boys' room fireplace. We lay on the beds—boys & I, and Robin finished The Big House at Inver & a Sherlock Holmes story. Very cozy up there. And warm with the wind howling outside. Left our *alien* books at police dept so we can depart December 2. They have to be written in —

UJ Friday Nov 22. 52° sunny in A.M. Rain in P.M. High wind all day. Boys played with ducks in pond. London paper says this is the warmest Nov since 1860! I wrote letters and made plans

---

[91] The "X" Una refers to was drawn several inches above the downstairs floor plan of Kerry Vor (p. 133). It is embedded in text written above the plan and is not visible in the sketch reproduced in this volume.

for our journeys. I wrote a long letter to George Moore & sent him 5 Irish pictures. Rode to Watlington in P.M. to shop.

UJ 45° Sat Nov 23. Fearful rain & wind. Garth got Donnan's complaint in the night & Donnan got a new attack. Had Dr. Edwards come. He thought it might be the chalk water. Kept them in bed all day. No fever thank goodness. Drew their beds to window and they read contentedly all day & drew. Nice fire in fireplace. I felt dismal. Robin read aloud a good deal.

UJ Sun. Nov 24. Boys better. Stayed in bed milk diet. Milk puddings etc. Sunshine for part of day. High wind at night.

UJ Mon. Nov 25. 52° Awful wind & rain. Duck pond half across road. Packed & got ready to go to London. Started at 3:15 in rain. Discovered magneto not working not charging felt desperate all the way—thought might stop any moment. Got dark at 4:15 so had to have lights on. Expected Maurice Browne to be there for dinner & dreaded confusion if we were held up at some place in the country—but we got through all right arrived at 5:30. —Browne couldn't come going to Belfast today but Bess arranged to have him Wed. Glad to be back at nice No. 7 again. Grand dinner pheasant & fine chestnut dessert. Terence[92] was having tea when we came & gave us tea. Bess came in soon. Percy telephoned. I called up Bert Gearing. She is sick in bed with severe cold.

UJ Tuesday Nov 26. Shopped in morning. Bought Robin *swagger* homespun topcoat & cap for travelling at a very grand shop Scott Adie Ltd Conduit Street. Also a beautiful gray shawl for Albert. Ordered Cameron of Lochiel for Edith. {Bought me some sandalwood at famous Bond St. Perfumers Atkinsons. It is good, the best I've had except my Chicago original.} Rained all the time— Got car & started to Canterbury at 3:30.

---

[92] Son of Bess O'Sullivan.

Almost dark before we got out of London suburbs then to our horror saw dynamo wasn't charging battery again. Ploughed along in dark with dim lights on & weak horn. Just a few miles beyond Rochester I became terrified about driving. I couldn't see ahead & there was lots of traffic. I felt we might all be killed or kill a bystander so we turned back to Chatham, which joins on to Rochester & put our car in the Ford garage at Chatham & spent the night in a queer old coaching inn "The Royal Victoria and Bull" filled with old copper & brass & china & all up & down little passages & stairs & old prints & mementos of Dickens. He lived near here at Gad's Hill & spoke of this old hotel in his books. Autograph letters of his on wall in lounge & autograph letter of Queen Victoria who spent the night here & changed her coaching horses. Good dinner. {(about this inn) "Nice place, good beds" —etc quotation from Pickwick cut in wood over door.} Castle & cathedral here. Henna sails on Medway.

UJ Wed Nov 27. Robin got up early & went to garage. They seemed efficient. Got car. Went to Canterbury. Carved gate leading to Canterbury Cathedral very beautiful. Extraordinary crypts fine stained glass. Thought of my time here with Percy in 1912. Started out to London on wrong road. Went several miles turned back. Battery not being charged! Very depressed in spite of charming weather & lovely dying autumn colors. — Got to Chatham. They took off dynamo again & this time I think performed lasting operation on it. Took 1½ hrs.
{On board Duchess of B[edford]. This repair was efficient. No further trouble although we drove up through Eng. Wales & Scot. to Ireland. Left it in good order.}[93]
Quick trip to London over Bexhill Heath By-Pass then Shooters Hill—over Vauxhall Bridge. River beautiful. Lights lit & reflections very lovely along Embankment & Grosvenor Road. I loved London here. —Then home to No 7. Maurice

---

[93] Una added this paragraph during their voyage back to America.

Browne for dinner just back from lecture in Belfast. Amusing.
—Looks a bit tired. Percy came in too. He is very dear. I felt
depressed that I had not made an effort to see him more. I am
really fond of him but my life is so full of my immediate family
I seem to have no energy left to contrive courtesy to anyone
else. He tried very hard to persuade me to go to the Gargoyle
with him. I wish I had gone but felt at the time it wasn't
worthwhile. He was going with several men—notables I forget
who—& I felt too indifferent to be charming to them. I did
look nice in my black velvet tho! He intends to come to
Liverpool to see us off. Bed late. Terence is here now. He is a
sweet lad & handsome—has a shrinking shaken look about
eyes. —He was in a horrid accident—girl who was giving a
dinner dance went out on balcony with him, jumped up to sit
on rail, fell pulling him with her and was killed. He had a
terrible contusion & *must* rest. —He is afraid twill interfere with
his flying success.

UJ Thurs. Nov 28 Its Thanksgiving in America. Rain in torrents.
Il pleut dans mon Coeur[94] —& it did to leave London—all very
sad. Boys & I went to shop. Bought them grand leather jackets
at Harrods & gloves & ties & for me amber & a wonderful
unicorn seal ring Donnan's eager eyes had seen in an antique
jeweller's shop. It is a full unicorn figure running a star on one
side a crescent-moon on other & two pearls set one on each
side of seal (cornelian) & a coronet above. The pearls are set
on tiny emeralds or olivines—the strangest ring **very** old &
mystical. Isnt it wonderful Garth found the unicorn seal in
Scotland, Donnan this here. Robin promises to keep his eyes
open in Ireland. To Kerry Vor in rain. Lovely drive tho'.
Forests beautiful. Kerry Vor at 5:00. —Reading & letters in
evening. Got our alien registration papers back. Found letter

---

[94] "It rains in my heart."

from Millicent[95] & telegram from McFetridge about car. Our last night at Kerry Vor.

UJ Friday Nov 29   Got up at 8:30 & started to work at once packing. Letter from Emerson of Gortaclee saying he'd give £63 for car. Said McFetridge offered to sell it to him for £80. 1—
Pelting rain all morning. Had a fire in the harness room fireplace & packed in there. Repacked & sorted 3 trunks & planned about all our luggage some of which I want on way to Belfast, some on boat & in New York & in Michigan. Plan to buy a trunk & suitcase in Belfast. —Newell & Revitt worked all day getting house ready for Dickenses[96] & their party. They arrive at 6 tonight. Got everything done & trunks off to Liverpool. Had to go to station to send them. Paid all bills. Left at 5:30, drove to Oxford in drizzle. We left the duck pond flooded almost across the road. Put up at the Clarendon a big expensive hotel on the Cornmarket. It was filled with Oxford students & their friends & relatives. It was term end & they were wildly happy. There was a banquet of several hundred students in one room (the Caledonian Club). Some were in kilts. Bagpipes played at intervals. —After dinner we sat in lounge, lots of magazines the children like Field, Country Life, etc. I wrote 5 or 6 letters—mostly business. Students got more & more riotous & drunken—the Oxford youth is not very inspiring. Undersized & unpleasing accents a kind of mumble. The hotel is steam heated & the boys had a grand scramble starko. We had a big luxurious room with lovely henna colored curtains chintz with birds & flowers. To bed late.

UJ Sat Nov 30 Up at 9. At 10 we went to Barclays & found our check from L.A. Bank. They have been very faithful in getting

---

[95] Millicent Murby, a writer and translator Una met during her 1912 visit.
[96] Mrs. Dickens (granddaughter-in-law of Charles Dickens) was a co-owner of Kerry Vor with Biddy O'Sullivan.

our checks to us each month. Bright sunny morning. On through Stratford on Avon. [**RJ**] {The Avon flooded yellow water up to the bridge arches and among the buildings. Fields on the road flooded. Driving to Oxford in the dark, Una was terrified to find the road suddenly vanishing in a great pool of black water at Cowley. We had to ford.} [**UJ**] Woodstock etc to Much Wenlock about 100 miles. Put up at Gaskell Arms. Called Peter Davis'[97] sister at Bourton Manor on phone. She asked us to stay with her the night. We compromised on tea. Fine old house. She looks like Peter but more excitable. Showed us over house & around kennels. She raises Cairns. We are to go back in the morning & stay for lunch & I will write more in detail after. Oldish woman came in to tea. She is a keen rider to hounds May Whitmore. Lovely tea all homemade things cookies & cakes & bread & butter & jams & tea & cream & sandwiches. [**RJ**] —Bourton Manor is "on Wenlock Edge the wood's in trouble"[98] — —Whitley—Lydia's brother-in-law—had a crise de nerfs[99] because his wife forgot to turn off the electric tea-kettle. Paced in a fury, chewed his finger, switched off lights as fast as she switched them on. She sweetly ignored him.

Canterbury Trip	Rochester
Britwell Salome	Chatham
Watlington	Sittingbourne
Uxbridge	Canterbury
London	and back to London
Battersea Bridge	over Vauxhall Bridge
Clapham	Britwell
Peckham	Watlington
Dartford	Oxford
Rochester	Woodstock
Chatham	Enstone

---

[97] Lydia "Peter" Brocklesby Davis, a friend from Carmel.
[98] First line of A. E. Housman's "On Wenlock Edge."
[99] "Hysterical fit."

Long Compton	Manchester
Stratford on Avon	Chorlton-cum-Hardy
Alcester	Manchester
Studley	Bolton
Bromsgrove	Belmont
Kidderminster	Preston
Bridgnorth	Duncombe
Much Wenlock	Scotforth
Bourton Manor	Lancaster
Much Wenlock	Carnforth
Shrewsbury	Kendal
Whittington (castle ruin)	Shap
Gobowen	Penrith
Llangollen	Carlisle
Corwen	Gretna Green
Conwy Falls	Ecclefechan
Betws-y-Coed	Lockerbie
Llanrwst	Lochmaben
Pass of Cefn Ogo	Dumfries
Colwyn Bay	Maxwelltown
Abergele	Castle Douglas
St. Asaph	Drummore
Holywell	Gatehouse of Fleet
Flint	Newton Stewart
Queensferry	Glenluce
Chester	Stranraer
Northwich	Larne
Altrincham	Carrickfergus
Chorlton-cum-Hardy	Belfast

[RJ] {Ancient schedule of fees painted on black wooden tablet in Bourton church

1/– for baptism, 1/– for digging a grave in churchyard, 1/6 for digging a grave in the church, 1/6 for ringing the bell one hour, 1/– for "churching a woman," etc.}

"Gaskell Arms" the inn where we stopped, very pleasant old place. Tap-room full of village life Saturday evening—we had little drawing-room to ourselves. Walked through the village at end of twilight—nice ancient shops and cottages—dark streets full of mysterious movement and secret voices, like Watlington. The villagers all come out like bats in the evening and move to and fro.

UJ Sun Dec 1. Uricon the old Roman city just near country of *Shropshire Lad* & Mary Webb's novels. {"Roman & his troubles are ashes under Uricon.}"[100] **[RJ]** —Bourton Manor—nice old place with excellent chimneys. Huxley the butler showed the boys about and Whitley showed us. Cairn terriers, yew hedges, conservatories, dynamo and batteries for light, motor-cars and trailer in their stable, no horses, old village and farm-houses appertaining, also guest and small cottages which he lets. 4000 acres **[UJ]** & 2 villages on property **[RJ]** Little church with two enormously old yew-trees, old Norman-arched doorway, old baptismal font with a square-cut notch to pass the child through. The church like a tiny appurtenance of the house, hidden in trees. Excellent lunch. Una was conducted all over the house, while I made conversation with the old man. We drove back to Wenlock to take the road for Shrewsbury, and drove through Shropshire into Wales. "Last hotel in England." Arrived an hour after dark at Batws-y-coed, Glan Aber Hotel. Rain just beginning. Storm in the night; noises of wind and water. {In Bourton church, in front of the altar, oak prayer-stool (foldstool) with inscription in silver plate— "humbly presented" by the Whitleys on the 25th anniversary of their marriage, second year of the great war.} **[UJ]** (Old word for Shropshire—Salops.) We liked the Shropshire country, hills wide valleys and fine woods. Very interesting architecture black and white (half timbered, stone & some brick). Much Wenlock very ancient village. Mrs. Whitley very like Lydia Davis. Very eager to hear about Lydia showed me old paintings &

---

[100] In her excerpt from the final two lines of "On Wenlock Edge," Una added an "s" to "trouble."

embroidery & china & silver & gave me many messages for Lydia—also asked me to take out some gloves etc to Lydia. — Showed me about a dozen guest rooms, "the blue room" & the red room & the Queen Victoria Room (where there were a number of full length portraits of Queen V.) etc. —There is much fine panelling and a fine XVII cent oak staircase which they got from an old house & installed. Superb views from all the windows. Very good luncheon topped off by plum pudding. One of the yew trees Robin speaks of by church was encircled about ten ft. up by heavy chain to keep the limbs from breaking when the snow is heavy on them in the winter. Near here is the place where Mary Webb lived and the country about here is that of the Shropshire Lad. We left the old manor at 3:00 & motored about 85 miles to Betws-y-Coed in Wales. Mountain scenery at the last. —Arrived in dark— Fine old sundial in B Manor garden curved stone. Whitley told us they were snowed in for fortnight 2 winters ago.

UJ Mon Dec 2. Woke to hear gale of wind and rain. Drove through flooded districts up & down mountains then by sea—with Conwy Castle across the water. The Welsh mts were fine to see cloaked in mist. Rained in torrents part of time but we were cozy inside car. *Sunny* in PM. At last came to Chorlton cum Hardy suburb of Manchester. Went & gazed at two hotels but they looked too dreary. We drove on to big Queens Hotel in Manchester luxurious place with big bath private which helped us endure the terrible black horror of crowded Manchester. Telephoned to Millicent. She asked us to come right out but we thought 4 too big a party to descend on her. She came to hotel as we were having dinner. Afterwards we went to her house for coffee. Didn't enjoy visit very much. Her husband big insular Britisher who evidently ~~hated~~ hates Americans but tried to be very nice to us. He is pres. of Manchester Library and undoubtedly widely read—but very dull & heavy. Millicent & he seem very happy in their life together. Millicent & I talked of my visit to England in 1912 and our friendship & our trip to Germany & the Tyrol with Gertrude Davis. Millicent does lecturing etc roundabout & has a full life. Awfully bored with this call.

[RJ] South of Colwyn Bay, where the old (and present) road goes up from the seashore over a hill to pass up the Conwy valley, on the hill-top a much worn, but perhaps not very old, embattled gate between two round turrets, beside the road. Set high in the curtain-walls between gate and turrets, four big stone tablets, yellow stone in white, each of the four inscribed, some of the words in antique spelling, others mis-spelled as if by a foreigner—a Welshman?—to this effect:

> I King Harold defeated hereabout by the Prince of North Wales—Gryffyd of Llewellyn I think—and driven back to Rhuddlen.
>
> II Hugh Lupus (serving under William the "Conqhoror") on march to invade Anglesey, attacked here by armed Welsh, of whom 1100 were killed.
>
> III Henry II's forces opposed here by Owen Gryffyd on his retreat from Flintshire, who retreated again and later made good his defence.
>
> IV Near this pass Richard II (inveigled from Conwy Castle by Percy Earl of Northumberland) was surrounded, conducted to Flint Castle, betrayed into power of usurper. — "From these circumstances it has been justly remarked that in no spot in the principality has more blood been shed than in this defile of Cefn Ogo."

UJ Tues Dec 3. Gladly departed from Manchester. This day we drove over longer stretches of fine smooth broad roads than at any other period of our travels. Fine sunny day and we loved going "to the north and Scotland" again. There was a chance to expand our lungs & vision again. In late P.M. the air was cold and keen the sky dull & heavy with a look of snow. The man at Petrol Station near summit between Kendal & Penrith thought snow very possible (They have already had some heavy falls of snow). We saw miles of posts about 8 ft high on either side of the road at about 20 ft intervals on right side tipped with red on left tipped with black as we went north to mark the road when the snow is badly drifted.

When I copy this let me note down in my memoranda about *hearts* the one about Sweetheart Abbey. (refer to Baedeker) — page 522

We went through Penrith at 4:05 PM and it was already dark. —On to Carlisle. Good hotel Crown & Mitre. In the Cathedral of Carlisle, Scott & Miss Charlotte Carpentier were married. Her picture coming down steps was painted on a panel in the lounge & one of Belted Will & one "The Elliotts & Armstrongs rode, —thieves all." Other pictures referring to Scott. —Very cold wind 42° outside 52° in our room. No steam heat! Hot water bottles blessing in beds. I have two rubber ones. Hotels furnish stone juggy ones.

UJ Wed Dec 4. Left in sunshine. —There had been rain or snow in night. We went to Ecclefechan & looked at the house where Carlyle was born in 1795. Tablet. Plain square house. Noticeable features: archway (under upper room) leading to inner courtyard. We went to graveyard by church & saw the simple (double) tombstone inscribed only with his name & birth at Ecclefechan and date of death in 24 Cheyne Row Chelsea London in 1881. There are 3 Carlyle tombstones inside plain iron fence. **[RJ]** {Bronze image of Carlyle on height looking over Ecclefechan.} **[UJ]** Sent a Carlyle postcard to Lehman. Gretna Green. —Just over border is a house where 10,000 marriages have been performed in the *Marriage Room* so says the notice on house. The blacksmith shop where so many marriages have been performed was further along & on a side road to the right. Fine country, trees & hills & untamed rivers then the sea. We like Scotland. This run was through Kirkcudbrightshire. The New England women we met that night at Wharncliffe Arms in Tintagel thought this the loveliest country they had motored over in Scot. or Eng.

Arrived at Stranraer at 5. Went to wharf & arranged to take car on boat. We could board at 9:30. —We went to "The Kings Arms" had a good dinner & sat by fire & read. Also walked briskly for half hour along dark streets. Several very heavy showers. —Took car to dock at 9:30. Got 2 fine private cabins & found the boat lying very quiet. Expect good nights rest. Cost over £6.7/ this passage. {Before we got to Stranraer along the sea amongst wreckage thrown ashore we saw people searching for treasure. A man clasped firmly a glass ball like the Postmistress gave us in Knocknacarry.}

56° People of here seem more full of vitality than in England. [RJ] The steamer unloading dead chickens and milk, loading fish etc., and coal very noisily. We went to bed at midnight, (the car was not aboard yet) and were kept awake by the avalanches of coal into the hold, and wondering whether each noise was our car, dropping from the crane to ruin.

RJ Thursday, Dec. 5. 50° At 6 AM a hand-bell rang long and violently. Soon we felt the engines begin to work and the ship to slide. Slept a little, then rocking and pitching told us that we were coming out of the bay. Quite violent commotion. While I got dressed we began all to be seasick. All astonished at ourselves. Perspiration and dizziness, competition for spittoons, but nothing to put in them except a little saliva. Soon well again, but perhaps because we came in the lee of Ireland. Next day's newspaper says that this night was one of the great storms of the year, that is some consolation. [UJ] {Fences down, great seawall at Carrickfergus down.} [RJ] Coffee aboard ship, soon we were driving through Larne to Belfast. [UJ] {Castle at Carrickfergus very grand rising out of wild sea.} [RJ] The good old Clarendon seemed glad to see us. Unpacked the car, then down town to buy trunk, suit-case, blackthorn for Praeger, etc. We've just discovered that our ship (Duchess of Bedford) has decided to stop at Belfast on way to New York— glad news—visited Can[adian] Pac[ific] office, and police station (alien registration) to say that we would sail from Belfast instead of Liverpool, as we had told the Oxfordshire police. Good-natured plain-clothesman said it would be all right. Our trunks are at Liverpool, except the new one, but Can. Pac. office says they can be got on board without us. Fire in our room in the Clarendon; cheerful evening. After all, we like dirty Belfast better than any English city. (Una would say "except London," but not I.) If I had to live elsewhere than on our Pacific Coast, I should try to buy a bit of bog on Fair Head, and live where the sheep cry, over the great precipice. [UJ] Left car to be washed.

RJ Friday, Dec. 6. —Letter from Emerson of Gortaclee—he came with a friend at eleven and bought the car, £45 first payment, to be delivered Monday at Cushendall. Then we went to Mullen's book-store, to buy reading material for the voyage. Horrors of searching the shelves of a book-store. Garth could find nothing except a book on farm-animals that cost 30/–; Donnan got a book about tanks in the war; I could find nothing; walked about streets looking in vain for a unicorn seal; Una as usual found an arm-full, including several that will do to read aloud. — — — Emerson of Gortaclee said that McFetridge of Knocknacarry, getting Una's letter first, offered him the car for £80, saying that he (McF.) would have to go to Liverpool to get it, and it would cost £12 to bring it over to Ireland. Emerson had agreed to take it, and had £25 ready to give him to bind the bargain, when he received *his* letter from Una, offering the car in Ireland for £60. Fancy the excitable fellow's state of mind. Evidently we could have got more for the car; Coulter, from whom we bought it, offers £65, but we shan't disappoint Emerson. Also it is pleasant to think of our car still continuing to live in the Glens of Antrim. — — —
After lunch we drove to Downpatrick and drove around the cathedral there. Flooded country, rivers bursting their banks, furies of rain and hail all afternoon and most of the night. No wonder we are such fine fellows, our ancestors having endured

the rigors of this climate. I love Northern Ireland. I don't love
England. But northern Scotland I might, if I knew it better.

RJ Saturday, Dec. 7. 50° We intended to visit the Antrim round
tower to-day, but Donnan is a little discommoded in his
insides, so we stay at the hotel and keep him in bed this
morning [**UJ**] with fire in fireplace. [**RJ**] Telegram from
baggage-master of Duchess of Bedford, our trunks are at
Liverpool and will be shipped. [**UJ**] Una darns stockings. Rain
all night and this morning clearing at noon. We bought 4
shillelaghs (bog oak) & 1 blackthorn the other day. Praeger's
blackthorn stick is having a silver band put on.

Emerson says Alex Martin is still "astray in his head" —that he
is quiet & doesn't give any trouble but very dull at times. His
people are nervous about him and talk of shutting him up. I
like the soft inflection of the Irish speech.

After all, Donnan convinced us that he was in good condition
again this PM so we drove to Antrim Round Tower. This tower
is a very perfect one, and is in the midst of ~~some~~ a private
estate. It has been closed to the public for several years but can
now be inspected 2–6 PM on Wed & Sat. 1/ per head. —We
got our tickets and walked into the grounds. It was a beautiful
sight—that gray inexplicable "spear" seen through the gray
trunks of the leafless trees. Behind it the winter sky of late
afternoon rose-pink and pale green low down, and gray above.
Great flocks of black birds—rooks perhaps swarmed like bees
about its head then swirled to the bare branches of the trees.
To the right a moon golden rather than white, in its first
quarter—it was almost dusk as we left. —Over the door is a
carved cross. A ladder allows one to climb to the door but once
inside we could go no further. We had read that this tower
could be climbed to the top but it can be no longer. The ladders
are broken and beams swinging in midair. To the left of the
door and around the tower a quarter of the way a tablet about
1 ft X 15 in is set into the wall. It seems to have been sculptured
and then partially erased.

We drove back to Belfast contentedly through the falling darkness. We saw much flooded land. The road is superb— they were working at it when we arrived in June and still unfinished when we left in Sept. Its done now. We went to Waltons & got Praeger's stick—the silver band is on—broad & beautifully carved with harp, shamrock round tower & wolf-hound.

[**RJ**] The door of the tower has two very massive lintels, the shorter—in which the cross is carved—above the longer. Both are cracked through—gaping cracks—though the stones are so thick.

Door-jambs and lintels of big squared stone, the rest heavy rubble, with many spawls in the chinks. All that I observed was basalt or similar trap-rock. Projecting string-course around the top, at the spring of the conical roof. Four small windows at the top, four or so somewhat larger ones on the way up. I suppose our last round tower, and a very fine one, though not so imposing as Kilmacduagh nor so well built and well preserved as Devenish. {Leaving the tower we soon passed two gate-posts that were exact miniatures of it—the same shape, the same mysterious venerable air, the same gray masonry.}

Going in to Antrim we saw again the fine rath and barrow with the arched entrance, that the boy told us had been used for an icehouse.

Delightful pilgrimage.

The hotel's only garage is under the archway into the courtyard, and a cat with innumerable muddy feet dances on the car all night long. To-day the wind banged the doors so that I could not stop them to get the car out until an old man came and held them for me. Then the banging had so sprung them that they wouldn't shut. The old man brought me an axe to hammer them into place with.

Sign in a shop-window just across the street from the Clarendon: "Adam Turner/Undertaker and Posting-Master/Shrouds of every description."

In Watlington was So-and-so "Carpenter and Undertaker." Some other town in England, "Contractor and Undertaker."

RJ Sunday, Dec. 8. 48° about noon. Home until lunch-time. Una writes 15 letters and washes a few things. The rest of us— nothing. [UJ] After lunch we drove out to Bangor over a hill road not used by us before. Cold gray day looked like snow— then back to Holywood to say goodbye to the Praegers. Old Mrs Praeger sat by the fire in good health seemingly. Miss Rosamund Praeger there and the brother Robin who does journeys for the British Gov't collecting data about flora & fauna in their colonies & also is in charge of trees etc in the Phoenix Park Dublin. He is a fine handsome looking man with an alert keen expression. We showed them the beautiful blackthorn we are taking to our Praeger. They wanted us to take loving messages to him from them. —Back to Clarendon. A little rain & temp 40° in our room when we arrived. Robin read Hardy's "A Group of Noble Dames" aloud boys lay in bed warm & happy. We sat by fire close by. I mended things.

UJ Monday Dec 9. 45° Went in our car to Cushendall, then to Knocknacarry. Wet underfoot but sunny in spots. We saw much sea wall down along the coast drive. Also many people gathering seaweed & drying it on the wall. Finally stopped to ask a man what it was used for. He said they still burn it for iodine. It brings £8 a ton. I was interested about this. —When I was in Ireland before I saw it being burned in Connemara. All of the motions connected with the gathering & hauling &

drying & burning of the seaweed (which they call kelp after burning) are full of beauty & picturesqueness. In Connemara I remember the gray sea & sky—the bare rocky land with sparse coarse grass & the piles of dark seaweed with the thin brownish-blue smoke rising & the figures of the peasants (the women in red skirts) working about, lifting and poking the pile. I have repeatedly been told by people since then that it wasn't done anymore, that iodine was more cheaply procured in other ways. {We saw two beautiful swans flying along low over the edge of the sea.} We stopped & gazed at Dromore cottage, — and as we approached Mrs. McKaye's house saw her band of turkeys pursuing & tormenting a darling Oswald Jenkins (boys' name for a duck) who scuttled about each turkey pecking at him as he dashed by. Mrs. McK. and Arthur McK. came out. They were genuinely pleased to see us. Left 2 books for McKillop boys. We inquired about Alex Martin. He is still *astray* in his head but harmless. Later we saw him standing in his yard pipe in mouth axe or hoe in his hand. He looked dazed. We drove on down to Cushendun. Very beautiful. We like it better with the trees bare of leaves. On over the mt to Ballycastle. Met Mr McKillop and Francis with two carts & small loads of peat, very wet. Mr. McK. almost wept, told of the desperate hard life of the farmers & the awful weather of the past year. His son Patrick leaves for U.S.A. next Sat to make his fortune. They all set great hopes on his venture. We had seen Peter McKillop inside the wall at the schoolhouse. He was too bashful to do more than bow to us. The schoolmaster Mr. Dougherty came out & talked about his brother who has lived in Montana for 39 years.

It was beautiful "over the mountain" ice in the hollows & thin crust of frozen snow. Loughareema the Fairy Lough very large and still in the cold air. The heather & furze bronze—the peat very black and pockets in it full of snow. To Ballycastle, past Bonamargy Abbey bought food for lunch & a bottle of port. — At Donnan's suggestion we drove over Aura Mt. turning to Armoy from Ballycastle and we saw once more the Round

Tower by the church & Robin got a fragment of stone. On then over the mountain. The road was white with frost and snow. Snow & ice lay in patches in the hollows, thin coats of ice on the pools. The heights were almost in the clouds—the gray sky hung low. Piles of peat very black with bits of snow in the hollows. As we went higher the air became more and more pure and bracing. —Far below the stream murmured—falling too steeply to freeze. We listened to the sheep vaguely bleating below—black faces wandering among the grasses & rocks. Presently a shepherd came with his dog and began to collect the scattered sheep and drive them in one direction. Later we heard that they are driven to the lowland farms when the snows come. This is the most beautiful spot in Ireland. We sat and gazed long—then boys got out & leaped about in the keen air. We opened up the port & all had a drink. Down from Aura Mtn & on to Black's Hotel in Cushendall—past the turning to Ossian's Grave— & past the turning to Knocknacarry. — Thomas Emerson was waiting for us at Blacks Hotel at 4:05 & we completed the transaction of selling & buying the car. {Sorrowful goodbye to our good car.} We then went to the bus & sat until 5 & started back to Belfast. A 2½ hr trip frightfully tiresome. Too dark to see out & the bus very bumpy. [**RJ**] Fare 4/– each! [**UJ**] After dinner Robin read to us. —Boys lay in bed after a warm bath. "Noble Dames" again. At 11:15 the Canadian Pacific called up & said to be at Transatlantic shed Queen's Bridge tomorrow night at 7 to take the tender down the loch. [**RJ**] (lough—we are not in Scotland.)

UJ Tuesday Dec 10. Boys & I shopped. Bought more bog oak things. Tried to buy leggings for boys. Went to Cook's to leave address etc. —Robin stayed at hotel & wrote letters & verse. After lunch I packed. Lots of planning to get things in shape. Had early dinner. We were very sad to leave Ireland. —Almost wept. —But oh so excited to be going home. I am quit of the obsession I have had so many years—The over-fondness for England. —Antiquities are fine, —old buildings & old customs

& picturesque houses & villages but they are not enough! Got to the Transatlantic shed at 7 —by taxi. Then began a tedious waiting. Only a few passengers about 10 I guess. Doctor there who looked at our throats & hair & eyes. —Said alls well. One Irish woman with 4 young children starting to Chicago. All children had dreadful colds & coughs. One little boy of 8 had right arm cut off above elbow. 2 children crying because chilblains hurt so. —Accompanied by several Irish friends to boat. We kept warm by hovering over 2 small electric stoves. Got on tender at 9:30. Still lay in harbor raining. Lights look beautiful reflected in the bay. About 10:30 tender pulled out to meet the Duchess of Bedford. Robin read "Laodicean" by Thomas Hardy aloud. We went to buffet to get hot bouillon. Irish woman & her 4 children all sick all over the place. Very tedious. After midnight we were alongside the great boat. It looked very dark & high as the tender was manouevered up against it. Had to walk up a very steep gangplank with all our packages. —Declined late supper. Went to our cabin. So few passengers they gave us two outside cabins with 2 beds in each instead of 1 cabin with 4 berths in it as we expected. Big fine white cabins with running water steam heat & electric fan 2 bright electric lights 2 wardrobes with plenty of hangers & big portholes. Cabins opposite each other. The temp. is kept at exactly 68°. We are so thoroughly warm that the cold of the decks is pleasant when we walk & we never feel chilled. To bed glad to be safely started.

UJ Wed. Dec 11. Woke up. Steamer lying at Greenock waiting for Glasgow passengers. Didn't get away until after noon. Extremely good food. —Everything spotlessly clean. Lots of space. Big comfortable lounge & large library. Only 22 passengers tourist. This boat has not carried tourist class before. It is on its way to New York there to start on 3 successive cruises to West Indies. Water gets very rough. Boat steady. For three weeks there have been terrible storms the worst say the papers in the history of meteorology. Hundreds of shipwrecks & difficulties, terrible floods, snow storms wind storms—winds up to 112 miles an hour. We are supposed to be in danger of meeting another storm.

Went to walk deck after dinner. Donnan slipped on wet deck and covered the back of his coat & cap with water & smoke dust. Made them go to bed—it was 9:30 anyway, & Robin & I cleaned the things. I am reading "Golden Arrow" by Mary Webb. It is very good. Late in P.M. saw Ailsa Craig for the last time. {We saw many lighthouse lights of varying colors and times of shining.}

UJ Thurs. Dec 12. Very rough all night. As we look out portholes we can see terrible seas. All salt water baths at 8. Robin & boys watch 2 little trawlers battling the mountainous waves. Showers & hail at intervals. Great wind whistling in the rigging. — I lay in berth a good deal but ate all my meals. Boys frolicked about deck in high spirits with grand little sea legs. **[RJ]** They played chess in the afternoon, their game supervised by a man—from Austria?— Hungarian, I think—who has not much English yet. A little shuffleboard before that, with Col. Cowper and R. The former is from B. C., has four children, but travelling alone. Ex British army. Was about to hand in his papers rather than help coerce Northern Ireland just before the war. Best-bred person by far in this part of the ship. **[UJ]** Boat so empty seems like a small private party. 22 passengers (even if all appeared) lost in big dining room & lounge.

UJ Friday Dec 13. Boat rolling badly. **[RJ]** The seas don't appear higher, but strike obliquely now instead of from straight ahead, the pitching is greatly increased as well as the rolling. We seem to be going faster than yesterday, too. The ship palpitates her little tail, when the stern is up. In the night at the peak of one of those pitches there was such a rending crash that I thought—half in a dream—we had dropped a propeller. I got up but decided there was nothing for me to do about it and went to sleep again. And once there was a great slap of water over the deck and our port-hole. Some of the dainty gulls are still with us. Una's bath-stewardess has mal-de-mer and is like an entranced woman. [UJ] Rough all day. Boys gave way & rested in their bunks & read for a while. I have read Sheila Kaye-Smith's Sussex novels, "Green Apple Harvest" & "End of the House of Alard" well written. & Richard Hughes' "High Wind in Jamaica." He is Percy's friend who was so eager to meet Robin. This book is really a wonderful study in child psychology—and—if they believed it—would be a revelation to the people who worry so much if a child sees an accident or crime or Blood! The tender things are thought to be so impressionable!

> "Some musky plant was enthroned in a painted pot. There were more plants in the window, their leaves obscuring the daylight which came through them like green water oozing through weeds."

So says Sheila Kaye-Smith on plants in the little cottage windows about which I've complained so much.

RJ Saturday, Dec. 14. We let the boys off their salt tub this morning, though I don't think they needed (or deserved) to be spared. They are happy all day—and not bored on a ship— They haven't very good sense. Afternoon and evening I read them some H. G. Wells short stories. Interesting but intolerable person. The crew have all been vaccinated for their West Indies cruise, and a few of them are hors de combat. One of the sailors told the boys that all he could see in Jamaica was alligators and black mammies. [UJ] Bright moonlight getting brighter each night. Beautiful over the sea. {A brilliant rainbow today.}

UJ Sunday Dec 15. Church in saloon below. We could hear the organ music & droning, through the ship's broadcasting arrangement. Water in big waves but ship steady. Last night we watched the waves as the boat racing at top speed threw up spray & foam & seemed to be going so fast it made one feel dizzy to watch. Boys played chess & shuffleboard & Robin & I read & copied diary. In evening we were all invited to performance in Cabin Dining Saloon—orchestra & cinema of Canada hunting, scenery & Indians & snow. —We were told by dining room steward that the ship ahead of us had radioed that we would run into a big storm. The library steward was ordered to screw everything down. —Just as we were undressing the engine stopped & gradually we stood very quiet. We thought of the two nights on the *Melita* when the boat lay to, fearing icebergs. I went into passage & a steward told me that our cabin steward was being operated on for appendicitis. After ¾ hr the boat went on again. It seemed very queer and made me feel panicky. —We had been to the surgery today. Garth got a cinder under his eyelid & I had doctor turn up the lid to see whether it was all out. —We saw the operating table there & the big lamp over it & wondered whether it was used very often. *Bright moonlight.* {I read Mary Borden's "Jericho Sands" not much good.—}

UJ Monday Dec 16. Gorgeous golden red sun this morning. The sea *very* calm for the first time since we started. The storm must have skipped around us. The steward is resting comfortably we are told—not yet out of danger. Forgot to say the old Frenchman who is travelling with (father I think) of the sensuous black creole-looking woman & her plump little boy—drank too much in the P.M. & got very excited sang songs & clapped people on the back. He wandered down to the performance in the cabin saloon & created a mild scandal. He doesn't show up this morning. It is a gorgeous day. —We are sitting in lounge. Garth wanders by & says Donnan is down in the cabin writing a novel. Doesn't seem surprised. Static makes radio news announcements hard to hear but we could make out continual rising of Thames.

[**RJ**] We went forward into the bowels of the ship to the baggage-room and it was closed. Baggage-master found at length, we got into trunk, packed away Praeger's blackthorn and a steamer-rug, and got out plasticine for the boys. They have had hours of amusement, since, modeling a squad of soldiers. Have also read to them for hours, more than half through Rider Haggard's Allan Quatermain, which delighted *me* when I was young, and is still pleasing.

UJ Tues. Dec 17. Temp 54° Running into winter this morning. Robin & I write letters this morning & boys model a darling regiment of soldiers. I have a cold. Robin finished aloud Allan Quatermain. I read Oxford Book of Verse. Letters. Down to baggage room again & finished transferring things. Boys threw a whiskey bottle over with a message in it.

DJ Wed. Dec. 18. Temperature 70 It was very warm this morning, and we woke up at half past seven. It is 16 degrees warmer than yesterday and the waves have got slightly bigger. **[UJ]** At 11:00 we went to inspect the kitchens. Very marvellous to see about 60 men working at meals: soups veg. pastry & breads. — Everything done by electricity even dish washing. Very clean and bright.

[DJ]   Dec. 11 — 189 miles
       "   12 — 231 "
       "   13 — 246 "
       "   14 — 338 "
       "   15 — 410 "
       "   16 — 345 "
       "   17 — 434 "
       "   18 — 424 "
       "   19 —

UJ Thurs. Dec 19 Very foggy. Sea rolling racks on tables this morning, whistle blows at short intervals. **[RJ]** Were told to expect to disembark this evening, "weather permitting," and if the ship should reach quarantine by six PM. Una packed everything. About half past five the ship stopped, and we watched to see pilot or quarantine officer come on board, but no one came, and we lay there until one or two AM, then crept in our sleep and awakened in a harbor-full of ships. The first part of the night we could see two or three ships motionless near us whenever the fog lifted. There was also a light-ship, pitching violently and hooting at brief intervals as if its heart would break—so despondent a noise. —We learned next day that the fog was the worst of the year, and a liner-ful of passengers was rammed and sunk near where we lay, just before we arrived. No lives lost. Fort Victoria, rammed by Algonquin. Also some trawlers went astray, one known to have wrecked.

Col. Cowper sat and conversed with us at tea—distinguished Englishman I spoke of before—captured Una's affections. They are so much more admirable abroad than at home—or else they export their best.

Una's long conversation with most amusing little old Scotchman, who unsheathed and displayed his claymore. He carries it on all his travels, with kilt, sporran, dirk, etc., to be prepared for any clan-gathering on St. Andrew's day.

RJ Friday, December 20 Quarantine muster in the lounge, called for seven, but the inspector decided it wasn't necessary. Breakfast. American citizens called to have their landing cards stamped—soon done. Then aliens, who were still being examined when the ship docked about nine. We were off among the first. Customs inspector poked a formal hand into each article of our luggage but made no difficulties and no charge. —Taxi to Grand Central Station—Una got tickets validated, checked trunks, etc. Checked hand-luggage, six pieces including Moore Hall-stone, at desk in station. Lunch. Walk to foot of 42nd Street "Tudor City" and back. Sight-seeing bus at 2 PM. —grand tour of New York until 5:30. I confess the buildings are grand. I forgot to say we admired them as we came up the harbor, between that famous sky-line and the Statue of Liberty. Intolerable quips and puns of the megaphone-armed lecturer on the grand tour. In his audience were only four others besides us four. Jews—Jews—Jews populate the great city. "Grave of an amiable child"—her father an Englishman who sold or forfeited his property and returned to England. Later wrote to ask that the child's grave be not disturbed; and the city has cared for it ever since. Reclaimed some of our checked bags, took two commodious rooms at Hotel Roosevelt. Went out for dinner. [UJ] Went to aquarium. *Very beautiful* exhibit! Natural deep sea settings (coral, seaweed etc lit up—very clean). Bowery with dense population & dirt & street shops. Brooklyn & Bronx Bridges. Tallest building Manhattan Bank Bldg, Chrysler 2nd was close to our hotel. Rockefeller's Riverside Church just building very beautiful. Electric lights & signs thrilled boys. Hudson River lovely as we came along just before dark.

RJ Saturday, Dec. 21. Long subway journey to the Bronx Zoo. Bitter wind and frost; except the bison, bears, wolves and some deer, all the animals berthed in their heated winter-quarters. [GJ] The elephant quarters smelt so that mother refused to go in but stood outside in the cold whimpering softly. In the monkey house the most interesting exhibits were the orangutans. The biggest one had worked a piece of wire off the front of its cage and was trying to pick the lock into the next cage. They looked much more human than the chimpanzees. The zoo had a fine exhibit of big cats, lions, tigers etc, we could only see about half the zoo because it was so cold and our time was limited. [UJ] A fine snow leopard & black panther & black jaguar & cheetahs. Saw a famous big rocking stone. Fearfully keen cold wind temp 22° New York to my surprise a frightfully *dirty* city. Back on very crowded subway & out for lunch, to hotel at 2:30. Found Jimmie Hopper there. He was the last Carmelite we saw as we went abroad & the first on our return. Long talk. He stayed until train time 5:00 & went into the train with us. The Roosevelt is connected by covered passage with Grand Central Station which is really a magnificent building. We were interested in the high vaulted roof with constellations of heavens depicted (with lights). Dinner on train. Sat in compartment in dark & watched for hours the snowy landscape which began 50 miles outside N. Y. City.

UJ Sunday Dec 22. Jackson at 7:40. Snow piled high. Papers saying deepest snow in 20 years. No one to meet us. —Telephoned to Mason. Violet surprised to hear my voice. Mamma had misunderstood the telegram & expected us at 4 PM. —Ticket man said he would make the fast train stop at Mason to detrain us— It left Jackson in 15 min but stopped after a few miles & stood for 15 min or more waiting for another train—the trains had all been held up. Some days no trains got through at all. Snow piled up very high, many cars sunk in snow, piled high against buildings, ice everywhere forests beautiful—snow under the trees & along the bare boughs. Conductor hated to stop fast train for us. Jerry met us & took us through high banks of snow to his house. Bright & warm. Mamma & Violet came over & we had breakfast. Boys were wild to shovel snow & played out in it almost all day.

UJ Monday Dec 23 Boys continue to shovel snow. In PM in 2 cars went to Jackson to Nettie Cochran's to see Max. Much trouble in starting Neil's car. Daisy displayed great perseverance & resource in getting it going. Very very cold ride. Roads barely passable. Saw many cars stuck along way. Max looks better but still very thin. Max and Gawn are spending the winter there. Home through cold wintry landscape which brings back such a flood of memories—not unpleasant very vivid. All my childhood winter life not hated then—but after all my years in California the snow is hateful now. I used to love a winter forest. Black bare trunks white on one side where the snow has been driven by the wind & drifts of snow beneath with pools or narrow brooks of ice winding beneath the trees. An occasional evergreen tree weighed down with a load of white. Tillie Mehan runs a restaurant in the old H. L. Henderson House. We had a good dinner there. It surprises me how completely I had shut away out of mind all those associations

I had with winter. Boys went up to school with Jerry in evening & got some books. Boys very happy. Jerry gave Donnan his set of war books & some farm ones to Garth.

UJ Tuesday Dec 24. We (all) are staying at Daisy's (sleeping that is). Daisy & Jerry are sleeping at Mamma's. We eat at both places. Marvellous how warm the houses are. In P.M. Violet & I went to call on Mrs. Moody (Zelle & her crippled boy Paul were there). Then to Mrs. Whitener who wailed on for an hour about her woes and Faye's faults etc. Also told us a horrible tale about the deaths of Mrs. Peters & her sister. Then to Rayner's saw Iva & Harry & Mrs. Rayner.[101] Very elegant & handsome all of them. Then drove past Rayner's Park to see lot Neil & Violet intend to build on (if V marries him!) Garth & Donnan had an ecstatic afternoon. Jerry got a cutter & horse with sleigh bells & they drove round & round & then went to slide down hill for two hours. I bought 3 qts oysters & we had a big feast at Mamma's. Had them raw fried & stewed besides heaps of other good things.—
Then over to Daisy's. Big fire in fireplace with cider apples nuts popcorn & ice cream & candy! Robin & I drove over for Neil in a blinding snowstorm. All the houses lit up & bright Christmas trees in windows. —Daisy has an evergreen on each side of front door which were strung with lights. The 2 big firs in front of Mamma's were beautiful laden and bending with snow & sparkling in the starlight. Packing & festivities kept us up until after 2 AM. Up again at 7. Golden moon in last quarter hanging in sky already pink in the dawning & presently a red sun arose. —All night the face of the courthouse clock hangs a gold ball above the town visible from Mamma's.

---

[101] The Mason friends Una and Violet visited or learned about were Mary Whitman, wife of Charles Whitman and mother of Faye; Mary Peters (wife of Henry Peters), who was an invalid who had been cared for by her sister Anna Howell for many years; and Iva Rayner Bond, her husband Harry, and her mother Augusta Rayner.

UJ Wednesday Dec 25 Merry Christmas! Up at 7, as I said. Jerry took boys & me, Violet & Neil took Robin to Jackson. Took train at 9:30 for Chicago. [**RJ**] Deep snow all the way. Lunch on train. Four hours in Chicago; went to Field Museum of Nat. Hist. and stayed until it closed. Splendid taxidermy—interesting collections—bronze Roman bath-tub ~~almost~~ exactly like modern ones in shape. When the museum closed we returned through biting wind and dirty snow to the station and waited until time to board the train.

RJ Thursday, December 26. Illinois, Kentucky, Tennessee, Mississippi, Louisiana. Until darkness fell in Mississippi, the level brown monotonous country was still streaked with snow, and ice edged all the waters. Darkies and mules. Breakfast in the dining-car; lunch of fruit, and nuts and fruitcake Violet gave us; dinner in dining-car. (The next day's meals likewise). [UJ] Got to New Orleans at 7:50 P.M. Our train the Argonaut out at 11. No compartments. Paid extravagant price of $73 for drawing room. —Went out to see the town a little. Walked many blocks along the main street, Canal Street. Street not very different from any other city except in extreme width. Down a narrow old street Rampart St. Rows of antique shops most prominent display an amazing number & variety of crystal chandeliers & sconces. A magnificent hotel *Monteleone*. Went into soda fountain place for ice cream & drinks. Back to station. *Fine bananas* for train 10¢ only for ½ dozen. —Just after we got in bed the train went onto a ferry across the Miss. River. Ferry boat was pushed rapidly across by several tugs.

UJ Friday Dec 27 We landed a week ago today. It seems twice as long ago. All day in Texas flat & dry with occasional swamps. Saw many darkies, palmettos & latterly cactus. Very dreary, poverty stricken abodes all along the way.

RJ Saturday, December 28. Still in Texas, then through New Mexico. At El Paso we walked about, bought papers and fruit.

At San Antonio Una wired Edith about our arrival time in Redlands. Must have been a surprise; we had given no previous indication of coming. At Douglas we walked about. There are two or three terribly tubercular men on the train; one looks as if he would die to-night. I have suddenly acquired the worst cold-in-the-head in many years, and am using up all our handkerchiefs. Beautiful dreary rocks, mountains beautiful especially opposite the sunset, prickly pear, agave, Joshua-trees, mesquite. U.S. inspector asking whether we have any fruit— quarantine against Mediterranean fly; but we have eaten it all. Arizona is much more beautiful than New Mexico (as seen from this train) and that than Texas. —The boys climb down at some station in each state, in order to have touched its soil.

RJ Sunday, December 29. We were to arrive at Redlands about 6 AM, and it is only a flag-station for this fast train, we were therefore watchful of the night, fearing the porter might forget to call us. Our watchfulness intensified by the accident of my watch having broken its main-spring the night before, rapped against the wall where it hung, by a jerk of the train, so that all we knew of time was by asking someone, or comparing the rare stops of the train with the time-table. —We awoke— toward dawn I imagine—wondering how far we were from Redlands. We were stopped at a big station—couldn't imagine what it was. At last found the name—Phoenix, Arizona! But that was not on our time-table as a stop of this train. We were much mystified, and only hours later learned that there had been a freight wreck ahead blocking the track, we had had to go backward and a long way around, passing through Phoenix. Were four hours late. Then our engine had a hot-box, a slow freight-engine had to be substituted, we were five or six hours late at Redlands. Edith and Allan were at the station; Allan had come early, learned that the train was late, gone home and returned again, but I don't know how long they had waited the second time. The little station is not in Redlands but outside; it must be a drive of fifteen miles to Fontana.

They took us home. By chance the Teaboldts[102] were there for an afternoon visit. Late in the evening we went to Fontana Farms Inn for lodging, though Edith wanted to keep us—four of us! Joy of Garth and Donnan at seeing their little chickens again. Edith in the evening stuffing the squabs for market, Porthus looking on from his perch.

RJ Monday, December 30. Allan came early to the inn and took us home to breakfast. Later he and Edith took the boys and me to an orange-packing plant. Machines empty boxes of oranges into a hot boracic-acid bath, then they are drawn up an escalator into a whirl of scrubbing-brushes, so polished up an escalator with arrangements for drying them, then they travel on endless belts to women who sort them according to quality; an electric contrivance counts the number of oranges of each quality; then they travel according to kind to women who pack them in boxes; then the boxes travel to men who put lids on the boxes, in three quick movements, then the boxes travel to a freight-car standing at the door; and so out into the world. There was also a set of rollers that rubber-stamped the name of its quality on the skin of each orange. And there was a man at the beginning, before the bath, before whom all the oranges passed that he might reject the bad and mouldy ones.

We went also to two hatcheries, where innumerable drawers full of eggs in incubating machines, temperature and moisture automatically controlled, were becoming innumerable little yellow fluffs of live chickens. Calm clean bright laboratory-resembling places. The machines make their own temperature-tracings—steady unfaltering line at 100° if I remember correctly. The chicks in the brooders run on wire screens, which let the droppings fall through, but I should think would hurt little feet. If the temperature drops a fraction of a degree, an electric lamp is lighted for warmth, goes out again when the temperature rises—a continuous rhythm. Edith also took the

---

[102] Harrie and Mae Teaboldt, friends of Una and her family.

boys to a chicken-packing plant, where the creatures are killed, drawn, plucked and packed, but I did not go and must leave them to describe it.

In the afternoon we took a crowded overland train to Los Angeles, had three hours to wait there for our train north. Took a street-car up town, walked about, sat in Pershing Park in the twilight on a concrete bench under extravagant banana trees. Except N. Y., this is the busiest, most crowded city we've seen. Returned to the station, had dinner there. —It has not yet rained in the south—dusty barrenness, except irrigated orchards and parks.

[GJ] While we were at Fontana Aunt Edith took us to a poultry killing and packing plant. In the outer room there were hundreds and hundreds of wire cages with chickens and turkeys in them ready to be killed. Aunt Edith said that some days the room was devoted to ducks and geese. The next was devoted to plucking the birds, hundreds of them hung on long lines like clothes lines. There were only about ten pluckers, but Aunt Edith said that around New Year and Christmas there was such a rush for birds that the workers worked elbow to elbow. The next room was the packing room with the temperature at about freezing and opening off that is the storage room with the temperature at several degrees below zero. The plant belongs to Swift. She also took us to an incubator plant where they hatched and shipped baby chicks wholesale it was very clean and warm. On each incubator there was a round chart with an automatic pen that recorded the temperature. In a little cage were some newly hatched chicks and we saw one egg just being broken. On the way out he gave us each a thermometer. The next hatching plant was bigger but practically the same in all other particulars.

RJ Tuesday, Dec. 31. Awoke in a greener world; there has been one rain here northward, though several weeks ago. Salinas Valley all spiked with three-inch blades of green. Change trains at Castroville; in the local train a Pullman car, "Lake Cowboy"

or some such name, that had been in our train to New Orleans.
—Trunks had arrived safely at Monterey, whence the Carmel
bus brought us and them to Tor House. But I got off at
Praeger's to get the keys of the house. Took down shutters and
opened the house. We were glad to enter it again. Hoisted flag
on turret; (and again the next day—New Year's day). No
breakfast yet; and our car of course needs attention, and
gasoline, before it can be used. Una went over to Teddie's to
ask him to take her to town. Schoeninger[103] came over here
asking could he do anything up town for us; I sent him after
Una to Teddie's, and it was he that took her up. She returned
and made coffee. We unpacked the trunks. I crawled into our
secret place and brought out the stored goods, Garth and
Donnan helping. Watered the yew trees. In much (but clearing)
disorder we began to live at home again. In a few days the tardy
rains began in earnest, we and the trees were well pleased.
[UJ] End of our Journal & of the year 1929.

---

[103] Joseph Schoeninger, a neighbor of the Jefferses.

1. Donnan, Robinson, and Garth on board ship near
Greenock, Scotland.

2. Donnan and Garth in Gort, Ireland, August.

3. Moore Hall, near Castlebar, Co. Mayo, Ireland.

4. Robinson, Donnan, and Garth at the Giant's Causeway, Northern Ireland.

5. Edward Martyn's Tillyra Castle, near Kiltartan, Co. Galway, Ireland.

6. Donnan, Garth, and Una, Cushendun, Glens of Antrim, Ireland.

7. Yeats' Tower at Ballylee Castle, Ireland, July.

8. Garth and Donnan in churchyard, Clonmacnoise, Ireland.

Robinson Jeffers' Foreword to
Visits to Ireland (1954)

We were poor, and had a house to make and two sons to bring up, so that it was seventeen years after our marriage before Una felt that she could indulge her dear desire, to go traveling again in Ireland. She had been there a few rapid weeks in 1912, but now in '29 she had a family to take along, and I think it was a joyous burden to her. As for me, I went under protest. I had never been in Ireland, but when I was a child my father used to lug me to Europe every summer, and then left me four years in Swiss schools: I thought I had done my stint. Nor did our sons have the least desire to see Ireland. They had no particular objection; they were twelve years old and darkest Africa would have attracted them; but why Ireland? It was Una's invincible energy that lighted our course, like a torch and like a scourge. Let me quote from her diary in Donegal: "Donnan" (by twenty minutes our elder son) "dreamed it was the night before we left home. A howling was heard outside the door. Robin rushed out, and soon came back, his arm covered with blood. A mad dog had bitten him. Donnan got worried and said maybe Father ought to have Pasteur treatment. Una said, 'Yes, I wish he might, but it's impossible. To-morrow we start for Ireland.'"[1]

Why did Una so love Ireland? Partly because two of her grandparents were born there, but I fancy they were Scots.

---

[1] Una related this story in the 1937 travel diary.—ed.

Partly because the bogs and the mountains are amazingly beautiful; and the Irish round towers, those hundred-foot-tall stone cylinders scattered all about the country, are beautiful and ancient and mysterious, standing on the margin between history and prehistory. Una wanted to visit every one of them. It was like a fox-hunt in the dark; for they are in no book thoroughly listed; and some are nearly impossible to find, hidden away in a voiceless solitude beyond some twisted lane's end, where—but for the masonry tower—you would think no one had ever lived or breathed. Yet we found them; we found nearly all of them, even the ruined stumps and forgotten fragments.

But there was another reason for Una's love of Ireland, and a more compelling one.—No: not political: she took no sides in foreign politics.—It was because Yeats and a few others, even George Moore in his fashion, had made Ireland magical. That was a miracle wrought in our own time, and without benefit of Leprechauns. No doubt the miracle is somewhat tarnished now, but it still trails a light over that rainy island; and the mountains and waters, beautiful in themselves and in their names—Knocknarea, Coolaney, Ben Bulben, Lough Carra, Galway Bay and the Aran Islands—have the added significance of poetry. Certainly the Irish seas are not the Aegean: but the poetry was exciting in its time, and much of it remains genuine.

Una had introductory letters to Yeats and others, but the letters were never delivered. The landscape was what she desired; we had read the poems.

But now I see that I must speak of Una as she was, before and after these diaries. She was from Michigan, and always thought it the most beautiful state in the Union. Her father, as I saw him, was a small tough old man with fierce blue eyes. He had been a sharp-shooter in our Civil War, enlisting before his time, at sixteen a killer, and had survived desperate wounds and Libby Prison, and was later the sheriff of his county in Michigan. His name was Call, and very likely Una was right in tracing his descent to the Richard Call who married—in spite of their objections—into the Paston family of Norfolk, writers of the famous letters. Una's mother was a tall blonde woman of great vitality and Scotch-Irish ancestry. It was a good union, and its daughters were beautiful. Una's ten-years-younger twin sisters have preferred to remain where they were born, in southern Michigan, but Una at sixteen came to California and matriculated at the University. She had a powerful ambitious mind—ambitious not for herself but of life and knowledge. She was very beautiful, capable of intense joy and passionate resentment, little of stature, dowered with great blue eyes and heavy bronze hair. It is no wonder that she was married at seventeen.

My first meeting with her was in a class devoted to Goethe's Faust, at the University of Southern California; for—as she told me later—she had stipulated that she must be allowed to go to college—part time—after her marriage. I have always rather disliked Goethe and his fame, thinking that Marlowe's Faustus and the Book of Job are greater poems than his great one, which derives from them—I cannot imagine why I was in that class. And Una has told me that she resented my presence, because I had learned German in Europe, and she had been first in the class before I joined it.

There were troublesome and passionate occasions before her divorce and remarriage were accomplished. Her first husband, who has remained ever one of her best friends, proposed that she go to Europe for a year—promising not to meet me nor write to me—and think the matter over. It was at this time, in 1912, that she first visited Ireland, young and alone, but most of her time was in England and Italy. She enjoyed her travels, I think, but she returned in less than a year; and we lived in Seattle until the divorce became final.

We were married in Tacoma—I forget why there—it was probably to keep my mother, who wished to attend the ceremony, from being affronted by the fact that we had shared a cottage—a pleasant place on the lake shore, where our canoe

lay at the door, chained to an alder tree, and the University of
Washington chimes rang liquid across the bay. Paddling in
dense fog on the wide lake, we had been glad of those bells to
give us direction and lead toward shore.

I wish that Una had kept diaries of that time, and of our
life when we made a home for ourselves in Carmel, loving the
sea-beauty of the place but knowing at first no person there.
There is no record but in memory. As to these papers, her Irish
and British travel-diaries, I am trying to choose among the
entries and make a small book, a mere selection, five percent
of the material. But everywhere her spirit comes through, and
choice is a fool, it becomes merely arbitrary.

I must note that she required me and our sons to
contribute to her diaries—and so we did—mostly to the first
one. We wrote because she asked us to, and our several
contributions are marked by initials at the heads of
paragraphs—UJ for Una, DJ for Donnan, GJ for our son
Garth, RJ for myself. But whatever we wrote is Una's voice.
She was author and recorder and captain of these little
journeys. We never went to the continent of Europe, because
she did not wish to. We always visited England and Scotland
because she did; but to make a small book it seems better to
omit all that, however reluctantly, and give the field to Ireland.

Robinson Jeffers[2]

[2] In Una Jeffers, *Visits to Ireland: Travel-Diaries of Una Jeffers* (Los Angeles:
The Ward Ritchie Press, 1954), 5–8.

Index

Dunollie Castle, 65
Dunseverick, 53; castle, 53
Durbeyfield, Tess, 112n78
Dürer, Albrecht drawings, 93
Dutch Flats (Nevada), 2

Edgeworth, Maria, 18; gift to Sir
  Walter Scott from, 77
Edgeworthtown, 18
Edinburgh, 74–76; castle, 74–
  75, 75–76
Egyptian schoolboy's letter, 104
End of the House of Alard, The
  (Kaye-Smith), 155; quote
  from, 155
English Minstrelsy (Baring-
  Gould), 116
Enniskillen, 24; castle, 24
Ervine, St. John Greer, *Ulster*, 6
Ewelme, 90–91, 97–98, 101–2
Excalibur, 119
Exeter Cathedral, 115–16

Fair Head, 17, 48–49, 51, 55–56,
  147
Field, Sara Bard, 105
Field Museum of Natural
  History (Chicago), 162
Fingal's Cave, 65
Finvoy, 47
flax, harvesting of, 46, 53
Florida Manor, 12–13
Fontana (California), 163
Ford sedan: Emerson of
  Gortalee, interest in, 139, 147;
  engine noise, 126, 127, 131;
  magneto trouble, 126, 136,
  137; McFetridge, interest in,
  139, 147; mudguards and
  hubcap damaged, 67–68;
  name of, 27n20; purchase of,
  11; repair of, 75, 104, 126,
  131, 137; selling of, 152; tire
  blowout, 22, 73, 102

Fort Quebec, 4
Four Feathers (Cooper), 88
Free State, 17, 18
From the Earth to the Moon
  (Verne), 6

Gaelic cross, 27
Galway, 20
Garron Point, 36–37
Garron Tower Hotel, 46, 52
Gearing, Alberta, 100, 111, 124,
  136
geese, 13, 28, 29, 44, 51, 53
German howitzer, 9
Giant's Causeway, 15, 65
Giant's Ring, 60–62
Glamis, 72
Glastonbury Cathedral, 127
Gleichen, Count Albert Edward
  Wilfred, 94
Gleitz, Mercedes, 54
Glenariffe Glen, 47
Glencolumbkille, 31
Glendalough, 41; hotel, 41, 43;
  round tower, 41
Glendun, 36–37; map of area,
  61; viaduct, 15, 32
Gobán Saor, 43; castle, 56
"Gobbins," 51
Godolphin Hotel, 119, 120–21
Gogarty, Dermot, 21
Gogarty, Dr. Oliver St. John, 20
Golden Arrow, The (Webb), 154
Goldsmith, Oliver, 39
"Good Stone," 46
Gort, 19, 20; cattle fair, 43
Granard, 18
Grand Central Station, 158,
  159–60
Grapes of Wrath (Cable), 6
"Grave of an amiable child,"
  159
Great Hall (Winchester), 112
Great Salt Lake, 2